D I S P L A Y I N G
PICTURES

DISPLAYING
PICTURES

A COMPLETE GUIDE TO FRAMING, ARRANGING AND LIGHTING PAINTINGS, PRINTS AND PHOTOGRAPHS

CAROLINE CLIFTON-MOGG AND PIERS FEETHAM

MITCHELL BEAZLEY

DISPLAYING PICTURES

Caroline Clifton-Mogg and Piers Feetham

First published in Great Britain in 1988
by Mitchell Beazley
an imprint of Reed Consumer Books Limited
Michelin House
81 Fulham Road
London SW3 6RB
and Auckland, Melbourne, Singapore and Toronto

Senior Executive Art Editor **Jacqui Small**
Editor **Frances Gertler**
Picture Research **Brigitte Arora**
Assistant Designer **Larraine Lacey**
Production **Ted Timberlake**

Executive Editor **Robert Saxton**

Commissioned Photography by **Peter Marshall**

British Library Cataloguing in Publication Data
Clifton-Mogg, Caroline
    Displaying pictures: a complete guide to
    framing, arranging and lighting paintings,
    prints and photographs.
    1. Interior decoration   2. Pictures
    I. Title   II. Feetham, Piers
    747'.3   NK2115.5.P4/

ISBN 1-85732-044-1

The publishers have made every effort to
ensure that all instructions given in this book
are accurate and safe, but they cannot accept
liability for any resulting injury, damage or
loss to either person or property whether
direct or consequential and howsoever arising.
The authors and publishers will be grateful for
any information which will assist them in
keeping future editions up to date.

Typeset by Bookworm, Manchester
Colour reproduction by
J. Film Process, Bangkok
Printed in Hong Kong

CONTENTS

THE FRAMING TRADITION

For centuries artists have used the frame – in one form or another – to define the limits of the idea they are trying to convey, and to isolate that idea from its surroundings. The frame is the frontier between real and imagined worlds.

Kedleston Hall, Derbyshire, was one of Robert Adam's triumphs in the integration of art and architecture: the paintings, executed directly onto the wall, are surrounded by frames in the same style as the room. An ornate flourish over the central painting repeats the motif of the elaborate frieze.

An image that lacks some kind of frame is an image unconfined – and therefore difficult for the human eye to appreciate as a whole.

That the ancient Romans understood the importance of framing we know from the evidence at Pompeii, where the many paintings, although executed directly onto the walls of houses, are delineated by vertical and horizontal lines of colour that contain the images and emphasize the story and design.

Probably the earliest true frames that we can see today are those splendidly caparisoned medieval examples, which are always an extension of the paintings, and indeed were painted onto the same wooden panels. The curved and vaulted outer edges of these frames echo the Gothic architecture in which they were meant to be hung. The rich gold decoration usually contained religious symbols and motifs that reinforced the religious message of the paintings themselves.

From these beginnings the frame played an increasingly important role, reflecting architectural styles and interior decoration. Indeed, frames offer a good visual guide, in miniature, to the stylistic developments of the time.

In the 15th century, subjects for paintings began to move away from the purely liturgical. Frames, in many cases, became less elaborate, and complementary to the specific painting in various ways. In the Netherlands, where the technique of perspective had by this time reached triumphant levels of achievement, the paintings themselves became involved with the frames in a conspiracy of *trompe l'oeil*. For example, the frame might be painted to resemble the window of a room, so that the image within

Far left The technique used to highlight this 1st-century wall painting from Pompeii is the basis of modern framing principles: the thick coloured surround brings out the richest tones of the painting and acts as a mount, for which the thinner white outline is the frame.

The elaborate, ornately carved and painted surround to this panel from a medieval Spanish altarpiece is a typical example of how frames were used in this period to reinforce the moral or religious message of an image.

This famous work by Flemish painter David Teniers the Younger (1610–90), showing the Archduke Leopold's gallery, is ornately framed – but with one exception the frames shown in the painting itself are far from florid. Their sobriety is typical of the Low Countries: in France in the same period a far more curvaceous style was usual. Among the interesting details of this image are the curtains drawn aside from some of the pictures: screening an oil painting with a curtain in this way was a common way of protecting it from the damaging effects of direct sunlight.

◄ This 16th-century painting executed by Italian artists at the royal palace at Fontainebleau, just outside Paris, is the centrepiece of an elaborate composition comprising cherubs and caryatids, all resting on a platform of ornately carved and gilt-edged panels. The initials for François I incorporated in the panels and the frame signify the royal sense of power and self-importance, while the moulded fruit is a conventional symbol of munificence.

looked like a view outside.

The Renaissance brought to frames – as to many other art forms – a new exuberance and inventiveness. Examples from this period are works of art in their own right. Many Italian Renaissance frames are particularly interesting, as they show so much of the architectural detail of the time. They also show a richness that parallels the glowing paintings inside them.

Italian Renaissance frame makers influenced French artists and craftsmen of the 16th and 17th centuries, when the courts of France were filled with splendid paintings surrounded by splendid frames. Rich, dramatic frames were needed to stand up to the strongly dimensional qualities of Baroque paintings and to complement the ornately hung and richly furnished interiors of noble houses.

In England the heyday of frame making was surely the late 17th to mid 18th centuries. Leading designers such as Thomas Chippendale and William Kent included designs for frames in their directories, but perhaps the greatest of them all was Grinling Gibbons, who with his limewood frames carved with birds, fruits and flowers and garlanded with ribbons, streamers and tendrils brought a lightness and beauty to the art of frame making that has perhaps never been surpassed.

The Adam brothers, too, were designing frames as well as furniture during the 18th century, and Robert Adam took frame design one step further when he began to incorporate frames into the interior design of the houses on which he was working. He went so far as to design frames that precisely complemented — both in style and scale — the pieces of furniture intended to stand beneath them. Mantelpieces, side tables and pier tables were all conceived with exactly the right architectural form of picture frame set above.

As the century advanced, styles became lighter and simpler. The archaeological discoveries at Herculaneum and Pompeii fuelled the fashion for Neo-classicism, whose severe lines were in dramatic contrast to the flamboyance of the Baroque age.

In France, in particular, ancient Egypt was a strong influence, with lotus leaves, palms and other eastern symbols heavily employed on frames. The Empire style, made popular by Napoleon, was ubiquitous. It was Napoleon, incidentally, who was responsible for having many of the paintings in the Louvre removed from their original frames and refitted with frames in the latest Empire styles — not always with the happiest of results.

The Industrial Revolution and the dawn of the machine age saw the introduction of mass-produced

frames and brought to the new mass-produced prints and the less prestigious types of painting a boring uniformity of style. However, later in the 19th century, a revolt against standardization broke out among many artists, architects and craftsmen. Once again, frames were produced for particular paintings and their contribution to the experience offered by a work of art was rightfully acknowledged.

American frames, meanwhile, had been going their own quiet way. As the nation developed, both its fashion and furniture tended toward a simpler style — one lacking the elaboration of much European design, and one that was identifiably American. Picture frames frequently reflected this simplicity. Indigenous timbers, often ungilded, often, indeed, unstained, were increasingly used. John Singer Sargent, a Boston-born painter who worked in London in the late 19th century, would strip antique frames back to the wood, contrasting with the portraits of pampered wealth within.

A number of artists through the 20th century, in both Britain and America, have continued this interest in the importance of the frame. For example, *The Owl and the Pussycat* by British painter Peter Blake is set into a copper frame embossed with boats and sun, which bear a symbiotic relationship to the fantasy theme. Some of the frames being produced today as integral parts of the pictures they contain are every bit as inventive and successful as those of earlier times. At the same time, with the development of photography as a fine art, a highly reticent style of frame, devoid of distracting ornament or imagery, has become accepted as universally popular.

◄ A detail from Robert Adam's work in Kedleston Hall. The fireplace, a work of art in its own right, forms the base of a pyramid supporting goddesses who seem to hold aloft the circular painting which is the pinnacle of this design.

▲ This glorious 18th-century design is remarkable for its equilibrium: the vertical elements, incorporated into a square, give an overall impression of harmony and balance. A series of squares radiate from the circular mythological painting. The whole thing is brought together by an intricate tracery of gilt.

▲ This portrait by Frederick Sandys, framed according to a design by D.G. Rossetti and hung on William Morris Arts and Crafts wallpaper, shows how the principle of designing frames to suit a particular room and picture was continued into the 19th-century, albeit in a subtle form.

Just as frame design has evolved gradually over the centuries, so too have the ways in which pictures have been put on display in a room. Picture display is a major aspect of the history of interior design, and one which the chroniclers of this subject have tended to underemphasize. The factors involved are numerous and complex: they include changing attitudes to collection and connoisseurship, and fluctuations on the scale of domestic behaviour and taste. Even attitudes to the family have played a significant part: in Victorian and Edwardian times no domestic interior was entirely complete without its collection of family portraits.

Historic styles of hanging often seem very foreign to us today. For example, in the 17th century paintings were often hung much higher than would be usual now — sometimes just beneath the ceiling. These elevated pictures were often canted, or angled, quite far forward to give a better view to the would-be discriminating viewer.

◀ Pictures around a piano conjure up a homely, early 20th-century feel. Although the frames are less ornate than in Victorian times, the tassels and cords reflect a long tradition of decorative hanging styles.

▲ This late 18th-century interior in Ragley Hall, Warwickshire, exemplifies the tradition of reserving the bedroom for portraits. The two larger pictures, in frames surmounted by symbolic crowns, hang from fine chains on a camouflaged rod.

In the same period, pictures were sometimes hung directly over tapestries, which at that time were often used both as insulation and decoration. Strong nails would be used fairly indiscriminately through the fabric to secure the often heavy pictures to the wall behind.

During the 18th century there was a tendency to hang pictures in groups with architectural precision – although early in the century it is surprising how often their positioning took no account of the divisions in wall panelling. One picture might be hung below another on a pair of chains. Arrangements were usually intended to work well in relation to the wall surface as a whole, rather than being designed for the convenience of the spectator: the furniture designer Thomas Sheraton was breaking with convention when he suggested that the height of pictures should take account of viewing requirements.

Arrangements in the 19th century took on a less rigid aspect. Pictures were often hung in tiers, secured by either wire or cord. The vociferous critic of Victorian taste, Charles Eastlake, in his *Hints on Household Taste*, recommended wire as being less visible and less prone to gathering dust. The cords, often single, might be hung from studs which were sometimes covered with silk rosettes or bows, the cords themselves perhaps covered in the same material. Eastlake pointed out the advantages of a rod fixed at cornice level: pictures hung from this rod on hooks could easily be adjusted until the position was right.

Toward the end of the 19th century, particularly in "Aesthetic" or Arts and Crafts, interiors, the easel was often used as a display stand for paintings, and became a decorative feature in itself.

After the First World War, there was a general pruning of Victorian and Edwardian clutter, both on walls and at floor level. Pictures and furniture were less in evidence. Today the rigidity of early modern schemes has been somewhat relaxed, and ways of displaying pictures are again a matter of personal taste and inventiveness.

◀ The tradition of hanging one picture on chains from a larger picture was once commonplace in grand houses. Also of interest is the proximity of the frames to the mantelpiece: the 18th and 19th centuries accepted many arrangements that to a modern eye might seem cramped.

This Pre-Raphaelite ▶ beauty (also hung from a disguised rod) is set against a contemporary Arts and Crafts style wallpaper. The circular gold mount has a halo-like effect — such reverence for idealized beauty is typical of the period.

Far right A classical look ▶ is achieved here by the use of ready-printed paper swags and bows which decorate the chimneypiece and appear to support the oval portrait and the ornithological prints. The ceramics are consistent with the period mood.

IMAGES AND SURROUNDS

Perhaps the most crucial thing to remember when deciding what sort of mount and frame to choose for a picture is that, first and last, it is the picture that is important. The role of both frame and mount is not to subdue or conflict but to flatter and complement the image they surround.

A plain room is entirely transformed by a wall filled with a casual but balanced arrangement of strong, bright images. Two more pictures leaning against the wall at floor level bring furnishings and images together.

A dictum that has become something of a framer's cliché – though still worth repeating – is that the greater the merit or value of the picture, the more restrained the frame should be. A picture not of the first quality can often be improved to a startling degree by surrounding it with an attractive frame that not only draws the eye into the image, but also confers "importance" on it by association or reflection. However, a significant work of art – in whatever medium – usually needs more sensitive treatment. The frame should be almost respectfully reticent in the presence of artistic merit.

The aesthetic principles of framing are more a matter of taste and balance than of rigid precept. There are, however, some helpful general guidelines that will simplify your choice of options. For example, it is possible to state some basic principles concerning the profile of the frame. This warrants as much consideration as scale, material or colour. When framing landscapes, whether historic or modern, the best sort of frame to use is one with a concave-shaped profile which leads the eye into the picture. If, on the other hand, the scene depicted is shallow or "flat" – perhaps a portrait or still life without much perspective – the best shape of frame to use would be a convex one. Falling away from the image at the outer edge, a convex frame presents the picture toward you, giving an illusion of depth to what might otherwise appear a slightly dull, two-dimensional scene.

Scale, of course, is also a major factor. Small pictures present particular problems in this respect, as it is all too easy for them to lose impact when framed according to conventional proportions. This is

especially true of small oils. The answer is to use a frame that is proportionately wider than you would use for a normal-sized painting. This ensures that the eye is sufficiently arrested, and drawn toward the image. The same approach can be taken with a small watercolour, but in this case you would usually need a soft, shaded mount between it and the frame to preserve its identity. Another option might be to make a virtue of miniature scale by setting the picture into a box frame, thus making it look tiny and precious – a jewel of a painting.

It is helpful to look at both the picture you want to frame, and the framing options that you are considering, in terms of "visual weight". The aim is to achieve a perfect balance. Oils generally give an impression of weight, as do many posters; whereas watercolours and pastels fall at the opposite end of the scale. A broad, chunky frame, especially if it is carved, is a heavyweight frame and would thus be unsuitable for a delicate painting with subtle variations of tone.

You must also decide whether the image is extrovert or introvert, pensive or deliberately strident, designed to soothe or to challenge. An intimate picture – perhaps a painted or photographic portrait or a domestic interior – needs a treatment that is gentle enough not to shatter the delicacy of the mood.

The colours of both frame and mount, in relation to both the image and to each other, are vitally important. Because the mount is directly adjacent to the picture, you must always take special care that the two elements work harmoniously together. Bear in mind that dark colours are visually heavier than lighter ones. If you feel that a dark mount is essential to a particular picture, ensure that the mount is slightly narrower than usual. A too strong band of dark colour can overpower a picture.

The colour values of the image should influence the choice of frame. Again, colour and proportion have a bearing on each other. If, for example, you have a picture in particularly strong tones, the frame should be proportionally larger to achieve a balance of visual weights. In theory, the converse of this principle is that a small picture painted in subdued colours should have a small, quiet frame; however, very often such a picture can look very good with a wide dramatic frame that calls attention to it, making it seem important.

The mount and frame should be viewed as a complete composition. Sometimes it is enough that they are complementary in colour, and harmonize with the picture they define. However, more elaborate compositions also have their uses. For example, you might wish to tie the mount to the frame by a visual echo of some kind. A good example is the use of a fine gold line on the mount to complement the gold of the frame. This effect helps to anchor the picture within its frame, the gold band serving a transitional role and helping the eye to make the leap from the outer edge to the heart of the picture.

You should also take into account the proportions of the mount. If you look at a page in a printed book, you will see that the four margins of white space around the type are not all the same width: to create a pleasing effect, perfect symmetry has been avoided. In the same way, a mount around a picture is seldom designed with strict centrality, producing equal borders all around. Instead, the proportions are subtly adjusted to make an overall impression that feels right.

The first principle of mounting – widely but not universally followed – is that the width of mount at the bottom of the image should be greater than that at the top and sides. This is to compensate for the optical illusion that makes any space at the bottom of a picture appear smaller than the space at the top. If this principle is not obeyed, a vertical picture will appear almost to be sliding from its mount or frame. If the picture is horizontal and the mount is the same width all the way round, the top will look unnaturally "heavy".

With care, you can exploit such effects to create an optical illusion that will augment, rather than detract from, the impact of the picture. For example, if the picture is vertical and you want to exaggerate its length, you could allow an even more generous space than usual at the bottom of the mount. It is, in any case, usually preferable to be generous with the proportions of any mount. A narrow one merely looks mean. As a general guide, a picture that is 8–10 inches (20–25 cm) in one direction and 24–30 inches (60–75 cm) in the other will require a mount of between 2¼ inches and 3 inches (6–8 cm).

This simple trio illustrates basic rules of proportion applied to the relation between an image and its surround. In the stylized landscape the mount has even borders above and below. However, the picture itself is positioned in such a way as to create a broader band of space at the bottom, which always makes for a pleasing effect. In the triple-mounted fabrics, note that the spacing between the rectangles is narrower than the outer margins. The colours of the frames and mounts blend with the tones in the images.

A watercolour is a painting done in pigments bound together by a medium (usually gum arabic) that is water-soluble. Lighter tones are created not by adding white pigment (as with gouache and tempera) but by thinning with water, so that the paper shows through. This translucency is a characteristic of the medium.

Initially, watercolours were monochrome – generally brown bistre, obtained from soot, or paler sepia, which came from cuttlefish "ink". Full-colour paintings were rare until the late 18th century.

Watercolours of the 18th and 19th centuries are usually landscapes, real or imagined, or architectural or else small-scale archaeological studies executed in quiet colours. Areas of rough white paper were often left visible, adding to the effect of openness and light. The medium has also been used for humorous or satirical social comment – notably in the works of Thomas Rowlandson.

Watercolours are not strident paintings: even the strongest images subtly seduce rather than brazenly solicit. The frame and mount should reflect that gentle feeling.

The first step is to select the right mount, as it is this that sets the tone of the picture. The Victorians were very keen on surrounding their watercolours with heavy gold mounts, feeling that gold upgraded the picture. Nowadays this is generally regarded as a mistake: gentle little landscapes in sepias or pale tones cannot stand up to harsh gold mounts. However, make sure, before you replace an original gold mount on a 19th-century watercolour, that the mount is not an integral part of the inner frame. This was a device favoured by the

▲ A traditional watercolour (thrown into relief by an elaborate wall treatment) has a classic gold frame enclosing a pale washed mount. The mount has been subtly highlighted with soft ink lines that blend with the colours of the landscape.

Victorians and should be kept intact as it increases the value of the picture and frame as a whole.

The classic, and simplest option for mounting a watercolour is to use a pale-coloured mount card in cream, buff or off-white, decorated with a watercolour-washed band in a light colour (see page 54) and then highlighted with a border of one or more lines drawn in slightly darker colours. This sort of mount will go well with most of the colours in the watercolour palette, and won't overwhelm the painting. A

sepia wash line can be effective, or you could try pale green; alternatively, grey-blue and soft russet red are both shades of the countryside that work well with rustic scenes.

A sophisticated variation of this would be to wash a whole cream or white mount with a pale watercolour, perhaps leaving the inside edge clear so that it can be picked out with a band of stronger colour.

It is best not to attempt to echo the dominant colour of the picture in the main colour of the mount. For example, a green landscape of trees

under a blue sky would look wrong surrounded by a bright green mount, which would overwhelm the picture. Instead use a sepia wash with a border of blue or green lines around it to pick up the colours of the image.

For some stronger subjects slightly deeper colours in the mount might be apt – a wash of buff or sand, perhaps, with a line border of reddish brown or deep sepia, incorporating a narrow band of gilded paper. Beware, though: this is strong treatment for a watercolour and would not work with one that has faded through long exposure to strong natural light.

A double mount is another possibility, giving a two-dimensional look not possible to achieve with an ordinary wash and lines (see pages 60–1). With most watercolours, the inner mount should be lighter in colour than the outer so as not to draw attention away from the picture. Occasionally, however, when the painting is unusually strong, the inner mount could be dark and the outer one pale – the inner mount in this case containing the image rather then projecting it.

A watercolour painted on paper of a darker tint, or one on paper that has discoloured to a sepia or greyish tinge, would tend to look dingy when surrounded by the conventional cream mount. In these circumstances choose an inner mount of a light, lucid colour such as light pink or yellow, making sure that it echoes tints within the picture, and choose an outer mount of stronger grey or buff: the inner mount will then lighten the picture, while the outer mount will contain it. An added refinement would be to widen the area of the stepped inner mount to about ¾ in (2 mm) and decorate it either at the sight edge or

▲
This period watercolour has been conventionally displayed in a narrow gold shot-edge frame and a cream mount with a pale wash line and a narrow gold border close to the inner edge to liaise between picture and frame.

▲
The soft-toned architectural strokes of this modern watercolour are well served by its simple classic mount and frame of limed and pale ribbed oak whose vertical lines echo those of the chimneys.

▲
A small, delicate canal scene is given significance by its substantial frame of heavy limed oak with a lighter, gessoed spoon moulding. An inner slip frame leads the eye into the picture as if through a window.

in a central band with a narrow wash or strip of gilded paper.

The frame is always more difficult to choose. A conventional concave frame, which will lead the eye into the painting, can be effective. Traditionalists will opt for a gold frame, which has a timeless appeal (see pages 66–71). Silver is rarely used, as it can make the picture look cold and uninviting. Even white gold is usually too harsh for delicate watercolours.

If you have a period watercolour in its original frame, and the frame is looking a little shabby, it is usually better to have it re-gilded rather than try to replace it.

Plain wooden frames rarely do justice to early watercolours, as the tones of the wood tend to look brash against the softness of the image. As usual, there are exceptions to this rule. A pale-toned picture might well take a light frame in unstained polished oak, as the graining and texture of the oak would counteract any tendency toward flatness. Another wood with good grain is pale sycamore, which can also work well with watercolours. However, you should avoid the darker woods, such as walnut and mahogany. (See page 78).

Modern watercolours call for special treatment. They are usually painted in brighter colours than traditional examples, and are often on a larger scale. The more definite impression such paintings give needs the help of a stronger mount and frame to balance them.

A favourite choice for many people is gold, but silver can sometimes work better. You can use a silver frame to complement cool colours such as blue or tone down warm colours such as red or orange.

If you prefer wooden frames to gold and silver ones, the same rule applies to modern watercolours as to period ones – avoid the darker woods, even when the painting is relatively large. Instead go for sycamore, or perhaps the almost-white poplar. On both these woods, a slightly rounded frame will show off the beauty of the graining. Another approach is to use a grey-painted frame.

Although oil was used in medieval times as a varnish for panel paintings, it was not until the 15th century that it was successfully blended with the pigment that enabled it to be used as a medium in its own right. Even then, however, it was still only a kind of coloured glaze for strongly delineated water-based underdrawings executed on canvas.

The growing availability of paper paved the way for greater flexibility and experimentation: artists could now try out designs on paper before transferring them to canvas. The range of colours, however, was still limited and adept brushwork became the most effective way to achieve variety of tone and shade. By the end of the 16th century until the end of the 19th, coloured oil primers were used over the white ground, usually canvas, to suggest, if not entirely determine, the final tone of the painting. The Italians — for example, Caravaggio — used dark red or brown to create an impression of warmth and depth, while the French favoured a pale bluish base.

During the 19th century the range of colours grew larger, and painters found they could get the colours they needed directly rather than through applying overlays onto a primed background. The development of photography around this time acted as a fresh stimulus to painters who were inspired to imitate the effects of light and shade over a landscape that the camera lens was able to capture. This new Impressionist style of painting, developed by painters such as Pissarro and Monet, required speed of execution and a greater flexibility of medium which was provided by the new ready-mixed commercial paints.

Oil painting in the twentieth century is no longer dictated by tradition or convention and modern oils have become virtually unclassifiable.

Acrylic paints are now also widely used. These give an effect similar to oil but their water base means that they are more adaptable than conventional oil-based paints.

Oil paintings are by their very nature more difficult to frame than watercolours: many oils are large, and the larger the picture, the harder it is to find a frame that works. On the other hand, your choice is made easier to some extent by the fact that oils have a highly textural quality, giving the painting an intrinsic presence which the frame need only enhance, not provide. This is especially true of oils executed in an impastoed manner, where the oil is applied so thickly that the brush marks are evident and are an intrinsic part of the finished effect. If the painting is particularly striking and impressive, a simple wood or metal frame may be all that is necessary, although such a painting would not be dwarfed by a more imposing surround.

The tone and subject matter are also relevant to your choice of frame: many oils, especially old oils, have a dark subject or background whose rich tones can be subtly flattered by a warm gold frame. Remember if you are using a gold frame that you can generally afford to be more extrovert in your choice: a stately and dignified oil can take a flamboyant frame with a scrolled, Baroque profile.

Oils are usually painted on canvas or a similar fabric, and held taut by a wooden framework — the stretcher — around which the outer frame is constructed. This can pose practical difficulties, as many canvases are not perfect rectangles and the thickness around the edges may vary. Allow for this when measuring for the moulding.

If you are framing an old oil and would like something of the same period as the picture, you may be able to buy an antique frame typical of the period and style from a dealer or at an auction, although this could be quite expensive. In large cities there are also framers who will be able to make a frame in the same style as the original. Remember though — the aim is not slavish imitation but sympathetic styling.

A 17th-century painting can have a modern frame reminiscent of the original: popular at that time was a

▲ Classic oils are usually best served by classic gilded frames. The large central portrait has a narrow but decorative surround, with a line of beading around the outer edge and an inner row of acanthus leaves. The smaller oils have frames contemporary to their period, grooved and ridged, with leaf motifs in the corners.

Opposite, top A coastal ▶ scene executed in oils is surrounded by a traditional heavy gold leaf frame, burnished until the ridges made by the overlapping sheets of gold leaf can be seen.

Opposite, bottom ▶ This Italian seaport scene has been splendidly framed in a gilded combination of a simple concave inner frame with a burnished gilt finish, and a convex outer frame with a leaf pattern. A narrow strip of beading runs around the inside of the inner frame, mediating between the delicate detail of the picture and its intricate surround.

convex black wooden frame, edged with gold beading. The simplicity of this sort of design makes it one that is easy to adapt to a modern frame.

If you decide on a new frame rather than a reproduction, there should still be some reference to the age of the painting. Any Victorian painting, for example, should have a properly gilded frame in simple style. Do not be tempted to economize by having a factory-made gold frame – the manufactured finishes of cheap gold frames just do not work with old oils. Opt for the simple and elegant, rather than making an unhappy marriage between classic and fanciful modern. Take trouble over the finish: old oil paintings must look as though time and care have been lavished on them.

If you are re-framing an old oil, the painting may well have to be revarnished unless the old varnish is still perfectly intact. The varnish allows the oil to "breathe" (which it could not do if it were under glass) while at the same time providing protection against dust, smoke and so on.

Some old oils are unusually small and it can be difficult to choose a frame that draws the eye toward the small artwork without overwhelming it. If the oil is strong, however, it may be able to take a more decorative frame than a bigger, brasher picture could. These pictures often look better under glass and an unusual way to present them is in a box frame whose greater depth protects the articles from the glass and allows room for air to circulate (see page 32).

Modern oils are, if anything, even more difficult to frame well than old oils. Colours are often brighter and stronger than in old paintings and canvases usually larger.

For the atmospheric type of oil that depicts soft landscapes and street scenes, you should avoid sharp, strongly-coloured frames which would look too hard. It would be best to use distressed gold leaf, or toned silver leaf – silver leaf with a sepia tone over it to make it duller. The frame should have fairly classical mouldings. Alternatively, choose a painted frame – but not one with a complicated decorative

finish. The effect should be one of a cloud of colour – a pale shade lightly dragged or sponged over a white or cream base.

Very often with this type of painting, a slip or inner frame is used between the picture and the outer frame to provide a natural break between the two, like a mount (see page 63). The outer moulding now distanced from the painting can be stronger in shape than if it were

abutting the picture. The slip should equate in tone to one of the lighter colours in the picture. Avoid brilliant white – it would be too hard.

For a bolder, brighter, more modern painting in clear strong colours and shapes do not try to use an antique frame, or a new gilded frame that has been distressed. The frame should be pared down and fresh-looking. If it is quite narrow, it can be in a dark strong tone but if you choose wider mouldings, the colour or tone of the frame should be lighter as it becomes wider. Dark frames work well with bright oils as the contrast can make the colours seem even more vibrant and alive.

A specialist frame which works well with modern oils is the float frame, which gives an impression of a painting floating within its surround (see page 165).

Tempera

Tempera paintings – that is, using paint made from pigments ground into an emulsion, particularly egg yolk – are usually treated in much the same way as oils. However, there are various technical problems peculiar to tempera, and these must be taken into account when considering the method of display.

Egg tempera takes about twelve months to harden completely, during which period it needs the protection of glass. If you wish to dispense with the glass eventually, you can use a slip inside a conventional frame to separate the painting from the glass until the tempera has hardened. Alternatively, you can make a display box or cabinet, larger than the painting, into which the panel is set. The box is then covered with glass. When the glass is removed, the tempera appears suspended within its box surround.

Pastels are a very subtle medium of artistic expression. Sticks of colour made from pigment bound with gum are applied dry onto paper, where colours can be blended or mixed. Their effect is beautiful — a distinctive powdery quality. However, the drawback is their dusty fragility. The colour can easily become detached: a vibration or a sudden movement may be enough to dislodge pigment from the paper.

If you are buying a pastel, check whether the work is fixed (sealed) or not. Some pastel artists fix layers of the work as they are finished and when the work is complete, add highlights to counteract the flattening effect of the fixative. Some do no fixing until the final stage.

It is common to commission pastels — particularly for portraiture. If you are working closely with the artist you should request that no fixative be applied. This way, the colours have more chance of retaining their original freshness. Make sure that the piece is framed and glazed quickly, before any damage can be done. It is essential that the surface of the picture does not come into contact with the glass, as the pastels might rub off onto it. There must be a generous gap between picture and glass, best achieved by using a double mount. The inner mount can either be the same colour as the outer, or in lighter tone — which is more effective when the pastel is on grey- or blue-tinted paper.

An alternative treatment for a pastel is to make an extra thick mount by sticking two mounts together: this allows for a deep protective bevel.

When mounting pastels, avoid echoing the dominant colour of the picture in the mount. The repetition

▲
Architectural images link these pictures executed in very different media. The central charcoal and pencil work, framed with classical simplicity, is flanked by two tempera paintings set in deep box frames which protect and promote them.

A tiny ink drawing is given stature and perspective by a wide white mount with a curved inner slip, surrounded by a lightly burnished traditional gold frame. ▶

of a strong colour can easily make a picture in this medium look gloomy.

Charcoals, like pastels, are dusty, and can easily become smudged or lose detail. As with pastels, it is important that they are glazed, and that the glass is well spaced from the surface of the picture.

Pen and ink drawings

Black-and-white pen and ink drawings need different treatment from black-and-white prints. A print is conceived in great detail and often worked on over a long period to achieve the necessary shading and nuances. A drawing in ink or pencil, on the other hand, is usually a far more spontaneous creation, often done in minutes rather than hours, to capture a moment or the essence of a scene. It may be used later as a study for a more complex work. This spontaneity must be respected in the mounting and framing, rather than crushed beneath a heavy-handed treatment.

There is no need for excessive caution, however. Many pen and pencil drawings have drama as well as spontaneity, and this should be acknowledged in the mounting. Double mounts are often a good choice, but the colour scheme should take into account the monochromatic nature of the picture. This means subtle contrasts — nothing too strong. A cream or off-white inner mount, surrounded by a fabric or textured paper in a deeper monochrome, could be set into a simple frame — in polished or black-stained wood, or perhaps a gilded frame that has been distressed to eliminate excess gleam.

As well as being executed in pastels and charcoals, drawings are often done in coloured chalks (which are harder than pastels) and Conté crayons.

▲ This large pen and ink drawing is positioned as if on a mount, in a flat stainless steel frame which reflects light and adds brilliance to the picture.

◀ A pencil drawing, strong in content if not in colour, is framed to ensure that it attracts attention. The simple gold frame encloses an outer mount with a soft mottled finish and a pink wash line, and a narrow deep red inner mount.

Conté crayon, named after the French scientist who invented it, is a mixture of graphite and clay, extremely hard to the touch and with a texture like that of very hard pastel. It is normally found in black or a reddish-brown, and gives much harder and more definite images than those of either pastel or pencil.

Drawing chalks are most common in red and black, with white used for highlighting; or on coloured paper.

These media are stronger in tone than the average pastel shades, and can therefore be framed and mounted with more élan. However, their textural qualities mean that they pose the same problems of deterioration. Because of their fragility, they must be protected from both dust and grease. The covering glass should not touch the paper.

Double mounts will give the necessary space. The narrow inner mount can be considerably deeper in tone than it would be for a pastel. For a russet-toned chalk or crayon sketch, you could use a matching russet mount, or a slightly lighter but still warm tone of the same colour. The outer mount might be in cream or ivory, depending on the tone of the artwork paper.

Narrow wash lines can work well, and should usually be in the same tones as the picture. Black wash lines can also be effective on a cream outer mount and can add definition to the drawing.

The frame should follow the same principles of colouring as the mount. You could use either a polished wood in rich tones (for example, walnut or maple) or a painted, lacquered or metal frame echoing the colours of the drawing. Contrasting colours will jar. On the whole, frames should be narrow and simple in shape.

Print making is an old and honourable art, practised through the centuries in many different forms. Consequently, this is a huge field (some would say minefield) for buyers and collectors. Prints range from the inexpensive (and sometimes crudely executed) to the rare and very valuable. By the end of the 18th century the print had become an important means of mass communication. Today, quite apart from the question of artistic merit, prints offer rewarding insights into other lives and times.

Prints are produced by an artist not working directly onto the paper but onto a wood block, a metal plate or a slab of stone.

The woodcut was the earliest form of printing. The parts of the design that were to appear white in the print were simply gouged out of a block of wood, leaving the image standing up in relief. Wood engraving was a development from this: a sharp tool called a "burin" was used to cut fine channels into the wood. These received no ink, but were used to depict the subject, which thus appeared white against a black background.

Line engraving on a metal plate adopts a different principle altogether – that of *intaglio*. A burin is used to cut a design onto a metal sheet, usually copper. The sheet is inked, wiped clean and the ink remaining in the incised lines forms the basis of the design. Early prints came in relatively small editions, because the copper images quickly deteriorated causing a loss of definition in the prints. After 1820 the plate was surfaced with steel, which held its shape better and allowed more copies of the engraving to be run off. Common variations on line engraving include drypoint, in

◀ An oval coloured engraving depicting a shepherdess is set into a matching mount whose colours tone in with the sylvan landscape. The effect is completed by a frame with a narrow rounded profile, lightly stippled in shades of soft terracotta over yellow.

This hand-coloured print of coastal scenery is again enclosed in a mount that echoes colours within the image. An allover pale peach wash is made sharper by a pink wash line around an emphatic gold-toned band. The frame is classic gold. ▼

which the image is scratched on a plate with a steel needle. Mezzotint (popular in the 17th, 18th and early 19th centuries) was one of a number of engraving techniques designed to give an effect of continuous tone in the attempt to produce more accurate copies of paintings.

Yet another method of print making is etching: a form of engraving in which the design is bitten into the place with acid. First the plate is coated with an acid-resistant wax, then the image is cut through the wax with an etching needle held like a pencil. Immersion of the plate in an acid bath is followed by cleaning off the wax; and then it is ready to be inked. Etching often has a spontaneous, fluent quality that cannot be achieved by line engraving. Aquatint is a method of etching designed to create a finely speckled grey tone.

Prints in colour (as distinct from hand-coloured prints) first emerged at the end of the 15th century but remained relatively crude until the flowering of colour lithography in the 1890s. Lithography is a method of printing from a flat stone surface by exploiting the mutual repulsion of water and grease. This is an extremely versatile medium, as the design can be applied by various methods – for example, by pen or brush – and there are numerous ways to create texture.

Prints today are without parallel in their usefulness to the enthusiastic amateur who wants nothing more than to cover the walls with good-looking images. No matter how inexpensive, they can look stunning when mounted and framed with brio. They also offer the opportunity to build a worthwhile personal collection.

Prints that are valuable should be

mounted exactly as they are: insist on this when you visit your framer. Cutting the paper prior to mounting can reduce or even destroy the value of the piece. If a print is in poor condition, you may be able to put it in a mount specially shaped to cover the damaged areas. If you want an inscription to show, a special opening can be cut in the mount to display it.

Decorative prints

By the middle of the 19th century there was a new outlet for the cheap prints that were then being produced commercially, and run off in their thousands. The print makers had discovered that there was a mass market not particularly interested in artistic creation or inspiration, but that found in the print a means of information, entertainment and ornament. The popular print had arrived. If anything, it is even more widely collected today than when the genre was new.

Diverse in method of execution, decorative prints also vary tremendously in subject matter — from scenes of exotic flora and fauna, to fashion plates, hot air balloons, cover images for sheet

▲
Top left Novel decorative treatment is appropriate for this humming bird print. There is an elaborate inner mount of gold and marbled paper, and an outer mount the colour of the bird's plumage. The wooden frame includes a narrow strip of veneer.

▲
Top Botanical prints in a soft green-washed mount with mid-green and yellow wash lines and inner rectangle of green. The frames have a simulated ivory paint finish.

▲
Above Neo-classical prints benefit from square matt-black frames — one weighty, with a narrow black mount; the other used unconventionally as a lozenge.

▲
Top right A print with a lot of blank space might seem to float away unless anchored firmly by the mount. Here, a soft yellow wash has a stronger band of yellow with ink lines in a supporting role. The frame, in distressed silver, has a blue band and fine red lines.

music and mouth-watering, luridly coloured mountainous trifles and blancmanges. They are brightly coloured, often amusing, and still relatively inexpensive.

Decorative prints share a strong style of drawing, and put over their image with refreshing directness. The mounting and framing should reflect this strength.

Choose a colour for the mount that echoes one from the print, and opt for something which is striking rather than subtle: the normal rules of tasteful restraint need not apply in the framing of a decorative print. The mount can be washed with several coats to give a deep tint, emphasized with fine ink lines or gold paper, or decorated by a technique such as stippling, sponging or ragging (see page 54).

When framing decorative prints, you can be more adventurous with your ideas than you can when framing a conventional watercolour. For example, if you want to use gold, a bold chunky frame that would overpower the average watercolour might work well.

Veneered wood frames come into their own with decorative prints,

▲ A restrained pastel treatment is appropriate for delicate book illustrations like this.

▼ *Below right* Narrative plates from children's books are often full of action and should be framed in such simple style to throw the drama into relief.

▼ The colours and shapes of these butterfly plates lend themselves well to drama. The ribbed frames include gilded butterflies.

and marquetry frames with their delicate patterns and geometric designs, are even more suitable. These were fashionable when many of these prints were first produced. Painted frames are also ideal for decorative prints. The finish can be a simple colour wash applied over an undercoat, or over a base of gesso. The frame could also be ragged, stippled or marbled. However, resist the temptation to paint a specialist finish onto a frame if you have already treated a mount in the same way: if one element of the surround is highly decorated, the other should retain a certain simplicity.

Period interiors
As the whole subject of interior design becomes ever more popular, the many antiquarian prints that illustrate interiors, furnishings and ornament are increasingly desirable. Chippendale, Kent and other cabinet makers published directories of their furniture designs showing in detail every new shape of furniture. By the Victorian era there were periodicals and catalogues illustrating every kind of furnishing and upholstery idea. Densely packed books of pattern ornamentation, showing 19th-century fashions in intricate detail, are well worth look-

◀ This print of a Scottish Highlander in a factory-made gold frame has been treated with a humorous touch of rough-and-ready kitsch. The awkwardly mitred corners of the mount and the stuck-on gewgaws make a calculated challenge to good taste.

◀ *Far left* A plate from a 19th-century book of ornament, showing Ancient Egyptian columns, is treated in a rich double mount, the inner one containing a marbled border and a band of gold. The primary colours were suggested by those in the picture. The gold frame is distressed over blue.

▼ This group of exhibition posters is unified by the choice of simple silver lacquered frames. Anything more ornate would have clashed with the graphic simplicity that posters such as these employ to put their message across.

ing out for as the basis for a grouped collection of prints. It is usually possible to find a recurring colour that can be used in the mounts to unify the group. If this common colour is subdued, it might be wise to choose a stronger shade for the mount to tie the pictures together more emphatically.

Posters

Posters may be regarded as a particular kind of decorative print. By their nature they are strong, attention-seeking graphic images, and accordingly require frames that are as simple as possible in order not to detract from the message conveyed by the image and type.

The most basic approach, suitable for inexpensive posters only, is to block-mount them. This involves gluing them onto a thick board and then coating with a layer of protective fixative, or painting them with several layers of matt varnish to create an almost lacquered effect. The edges of a block mount are usually coloured to contrast or co-ordinate with the dominant colours of the poster.

Other sorts of frame that work well with posters include the simple clip frame and, more interestingly, the wide variety of metal frames that are now available. The latter are especially suitable for large posters as they are quite strong and provide a narrow line of definition that contains the image without competing with it. Various attractive finishes are available, including deep red and bronze.

Many posters are very large, which means that you must carefully take into account the weight of an appropriate frame. Wooden frames are strong and can be reinforced at the back if necessary. Pale woods are too light for such large images: black is usually a safe choice; gilded frames can also be apt.

Black and white prints – a collecting area dominated by the highly popular category of architectural prints – require a subtle touch to display them to best advantage.

A rule for monochrome prints generally is that nothing in the colour of the mount should outweigh the delicacy of the tones. Rather than a strongly coloured mount. the preference is for a warm neutral finish – such as cream. sand or pale sepia. There is a place here. if you wish. for a thin wash line on the mount. but the colour should be soft: instead of a contrasting colour use a warm sepia. or something similar. These general principles are useful guidelines for most monochrome subjects. However. special considerations apply when the subject is architectural.

The term "architectural prints" encompasses a vast variety – from romanticized 17th- and 18th-century images of ruined edifices and lost cities to more factual drawings of buildings. whether proposed or existing. Details. such as doorways and windows. are also found in great numbers.

Such prints are often highly atmospheric. and have altogether a different style from the "decorative" prints described on pages 25–6 although the smaller examples do tend to look best in groups that make a strong decorative impact. These prints have definite vertical lines incorporated into their composition. and often strong toning to give definition: any wash lines used on the mounts must therefore be fairly bold if they are to make a significant contribution.

Marbled papers are often appropriately used in mounting architectural prints. Be bold: but don't spoil the effect by using the wrong colour of marbling. The tones of the design should tie in with the colours within the picture.

A double mount can look very smart – perhaps an inner mount of pale grey and an outer one of darker grey. all set off by a silver frame to convey the ultimate in subtlety. An

▲
Above right This architectural ruin in a delicate sepia tone is flattered by a frame finished in porphyry and an elaborate dark brown mount, ragged, with two fine stripes of marbled paper, fine terracotta ink lines and a band of gold. The overall effect adds depth to the picture.

alternative approach to a double mount would be to wrap the outer mount in Japanese paper. The colours that are found in Japanese papers are completely different from those in European papers – a subtle textured range that many people will find totally surprising. Italian tinted papers can also be effective. Or you could cover one of the mounts in silk or linen for a pleasing contrast of textures.

If your print is in especially strong tones, as many modern architectural prints are, you can sometimes afford to choose a less reticent mount and also use a much stronger frame than you might for, say, a watercolour. Plain white or off-white mount boards are too strong and do not work very well with old black and white prints, but can look very effective with modern ones where the contrast within the image is starker.

On any old print an aggressively modern frame will not work. Instead use a narrow distressed gold frame or a medium-toned polished wood – walnut perhaps.

Linen board is a good alternative for the mount. The linen has an interesting texture that affects the tone, and the depth of colour is quite different from that of a conventional board mount.

Although most architectural prints are in tones of blacks and greys, or sepias, some are in much brighter, clearer colours – for example, those showing Renaissance ceiling designs, Victorian wallpaper borders or French carpet patterns. These subjects call for a strong (but not too dark) mount colour such as bottle green or clear cerulean blue.

Silhouettes are the obvious representative of a whole group of black and white images in which dense black makes a strong graphic impact. The approach you take will depend on style and scale. One option (illustrated, right) is to go for a heavy black frame with a glimmer of gold. To complement the graphic outline of a silhouetted portrait you could choose a striking shape for the frame, such as a circle.

Far left A print of a triumphal arch, subtly mounted with pale wash and ink lines and a narrow band of gold that connects with the gold bevelled edge of the lightly marbled frame.

This is a striking and sophisticated treatment for a Neo-classical black and white print. The mount has a buttermilk wash and an unusually strong inner band of fantasy marbling that picks up the grey marbled frame. The red and blue ink lines are a bold touch.

▲ Silhouettes are the most dramatic of all black and white images, and look good severely framed in black stained or lacquered wood, with just a glimmer of gold. Colour in the ropes and rosettes makes a striking impression.

◄ A group of black and white architectural details is sensitively projected in mounts of creamy yellow, which is not as harsh as white would be. Frames of pale polished wood harmonize well.

Photographs have become a serious art form in their own right, and it is important to frame them correctly. The classic and still most effective treatment for a black and white print is to place it within a really large white mount. Whereas a black and white engraving or etching may be improved by the tones of a coloured mount, a monochrome photograph will not: an area of adjacent colour would only tend to distract from the tonal qualities of the work itself.

For a serious still life or landscape photograph in black and white, the only alternative to a white mount would be a grey one – particularly a pale grey, although it could range in depth to a medium or even slate grey, depending on the tone of the particular photograph.

The frame, which should be kept simple to draw the eye into the image, may be of wood or metal. Metal frames of various alloys are available in gun-metal shades as well as bronze, blue-silver and a very elegant grey-silver – any of these work well with photographs. Avoid metals which are too shiny, as these will distract from the picture.

Despite the wide range of coloured frames available, simple black is usually the best choice, although a more unusual option might be charcoal grey or dull silver. If you insist on colour, it should be very subdued – something like a deep mahogany brown or dark claret, or perhaps a very dark midnight blue or deep bottle green, both of which have hidden depths and will complement the photograph.

Old monochrome photographs, whether studio shots, landscapes or snaps, look best framed with old wood – particularly when they are sepia-toned. Mahogany is the ob-

▲
The perfect pictures for a monochrome room, these black and white photos have been classically mounted in large plain white surrounds with a white frame so unobtrusive as to be almost invisible against the white background, allowing the images to make a really vibrant statement.

vious choice, but other polished dark woods such as walnut can be extremely effective. High-quality veneered frames are popular again, and a good framer will have several for you to choose from.

If you are putting a mount around an old sepia photograph of this type, it would be wrong to use white, which would merely make the image look faded. A neutral shade is better, but not so neutral that the mount and the photograph merge into one another. An effective way to avoid this, and nicely set off the picture at the same time, is to use a thin inner mount in a rich colour and an outer mount in a brownish tone. If by chance the sepia print has been well looked after and its tones are as rich as when they first saw the light of day, a warm reddish-brown mount would enhance its glories.

For those inclined to experiment, alternative colours for the mount could include dark blue-green or even a rich burgundy. This last suggestion, however, is difficult to do well, as it can as easily kill an old photo as set it off to advantage.

Photographs in colour are very difficult to display convincingly. Most are too vibrant and full of life – which makes it very hard to give them a suitably decorative surround. If the colours are subdued, a white or grey mount will probably work; if they are bright, sometimes a narrow, dark mount can be effective.

For portraits, particularly of children, a blue mount, though not an obvious choice, can be surprisingly successful.

While a wood frame can ruin a black and white photograph, it can look rather effective with a colour print – provided that it has a fairly simple shape.

▲
The collage of photos is unmounted but contained by a minimal frame the same size as that of the monochrome photographic study alongside. This successful blend of black and white with colour pictures depends on the limited range of tones in the colour images: there are no bright colours to create a discordant effect. A collection has begun on the other wall, arranged around a blank square, the images large enough to stand unframed.

Tapestries, embroideries and other fabric works can be framed in the conventional way or attached to a stretcher in the manner of an oil painting and then framed, with a slip or inner frame to keep the fabric away from the glass. The slip can either be covered with a material that is in sharp contrast to the framed fabric, or with a textured paper that complements the textile. Some fabric may not need the support of a frame and you may decide to attach it directly to the wall on hooks or a batten. However, this would not be suitable for a delicate work that may deteriorate or fray.

Textiles can be framed in a shadow box – so called because it is constructed in such a way that, when it is lit from an angle, the raised sides of the display frame will highlight and shadow the fabric (or object) within the frame. It is a conventional frame with a deeper insert to allow the glass to be raised away from the base. The base can be covered in a fabric chosen to highlight the piece displayed.

The shadow box is also suitable for objects. In almost every house there are small ornaments that are not shown to best effect when left on a shelf or table. They might be a collection of coins, medals, old scarabs or seals, shells and corals — anything that is small, detailed and requires close attention. Fragile dried flowers, leaves or a delicate fan are also suitable candidates for three-dimensional framing as they need to be protected as well as displayed.

If the objects to be framed are intricate and the fabric used to back them is richly textured, then the frame itself should be simple. In any case with this type of frame, when the attention is centred on the three-dimensional aspect of the image, the frame is best left simple.

▲
These almost luminous fabric birds with their own mount-like stripes need only the simplest flat gold frame.

This wool tapestry by artist Phoebe Hart is designed to be hung on a pole and has an inbuilt gold band that acts as a frame. ►

Supported by battens, this ► weaving is in strong enough contrast to the wall not to need framing, although definition is provided by the black frames of the prints.

Individual items — whether these are small objects, photographs, or a collection of miniatures — do not always need to be separately displayed: small works often look good together within one mount and frame. The amount of space between the items will determine whether the group is viewed as a whole or as separate entities. If they are to be perceived as one, allow only a small gap between them and tie the group together with a strong ink line. If the pictures are contained within one mount but you want them to be seen separately, leave a generous gap between them and border each one with an ink line to emphasize its separateness. The colour of the mount should be restrained, the decorative interest coming from the ink lines. Where there are two pictures within one mount. leave less mount between them than between the edge of each picture and the edges of the mount.

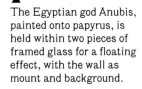

▲
The Egyptian god Anubis, painted onto papyrus, is held within two pieces of framed glass for a floating effect, with the wall as mount and background.

▲
Centre This fabric mouse is set into a box frame with a patterned fabric inner slip to ease the transition between pale softness and dark frame.

▲
Top left The heaviness of this deep antique silver clock case serves to emphasize the delicacy of the Victorian valentine within.

▲
These prints are held by a single black spattered gold frame and complex double mount containing two marbled bands and concentric ink lines.

▲
Top Three pairs of Indian miniatures are encased by deep oval cut-outs in mounts covered with raw silk. Simple terracotta lacquer frames attract attention and provide strong definition.

▲
Plaster medallions sit against warm blue fabric that emphasizes their fragility.

THE
PROFESSIONALS
AT HOME

Professionals who work with design develop an
instinct for good-looking interiors, often after
years of involvement with houses of many periods
and styles. Experience gives them both the
confidence and the imagination to experiment
with new schemes and even overthrow convention
in favour of originality and style. These pages
show how seven professionals – all experts in
their field – frame and display pictures in their
own homes.

The red room in
Christophe Gollut's
apartment makes its
statement with unwavering
conviction, yet without
being overpowering –
thanks to a dense
collection of prints and
paintings, focused on a
large classic oil, which
breaks up the wall area
right up to cornice level.

Christophe Gollut is one of today's bright young interior designers. Although based in London, he works throughout Europe, creating in many of his interiors a mood that is comfortably luxurious but without being slavishly tied to the past. Periods and styles are freely mixed, in a chemistry that usually includes an ingredient of the unexpected. This applies particularly to his picture arrangements as well as to more permanent aspects of interior design.

Gollut's own London apartment, illustrated here and on the previous pages, exemplifies his approach. It consists of two bedsitting rooms – one predominantly red and one blue and white. In each room pictures are used strikingly but without ostentation, reinforcing a mood of intimacy – the impression of a personalized space, filled with long-collected objects. In the blue room the feeling is light and sophisticated, with oval portraits and a mirror-picture of ruins set off against a wall of blue chintz quilted in one-inch stripes. The red room, by contrast, has a rich Oriental feel, with a Chinese watercolour, unusually placed against the window shutter, as a focal point.

Another example of Christophe Gollut's designs appears on page 114.

◀ Candles and a lamp throw this fascinating corner into half-light. Against the wall is a panel from an Oriental screen, against which leans a landscape in a red and white painted frame. The candles function as a kind of barrier, but one which highlights rather than hides the painting.

▲ This treatment is unexpected but exactly right for its context. One of the never-opened shutters has an 18th-century Chinese watercolour hung with seeming casualness on the shutter bar. A trunk used as a table continues the casual tone of this arrangement.

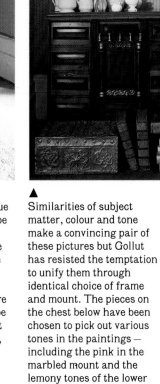

▲
The centrepiece of the blue room is a ruined landscape in a frame with a three-panel mirror. Linking the mirror to the mantelpiece is a 19th-century columnar clock. The oval portraits on either side are matched in size and shape but are radically different in decoration — one plain, the other ornate. Other pictures of varying sizes complete the effect of disciplined profusion.

▲
Similarities of subject matter, colour and tone make a convincing pair of these pictures but Gollut has resisted the temptation to unify them through identical choice of frame and mount. The pieces on the chest below have been chosen to pick out various tones in the paintings — including the pink in the marbled mount and the lemony tones of the lower picture.

erek Frost is one of a new breed of young international interior designers who can confidently mix periods and styles to create effects that are calculated but also seem almost informal. The arrangement — or non-arrangement — of pictures in his London home, shown here, reflects his talent for visual surprises.

Around every angle there is a view, and more often than not that view contains a picture which may be framed or unframed, hung on a wall or propped to suggest a flexible display. Derek Frost knows a good deal about art and appreciates its form and place in interior design.

The eclecticism of the work he displays owes something to the nature of his design projects, which take him constantly from London to New York, to Africa, or to South-East Asia. An equally important influence on his choice and arrangement of art is the character of his furniture and of the light-flooded rooms, halls and curving stairways and galleries in his home.

Much of the furniture is designed by Frost himself, using craftsmen who have brought old skills such as marquetry and inlay work to his highly individual pieces. Each piece of furniture stands on its own merits, seemingly independent of its surroundings, which might be modern steel or period marble. The pictures are therefore arranged to work with these unusually significant objects. There are no compromises: this modern classicism is a look you either accept or reject, but one which certainly engages your attention.

More of Derek Frost's designs appear on pages 14-15; 16; 32 (bottom right); 54; 102; 106-7; 109; 117 (bottom right); 121; 135 (right); 140 (right).

◀ In the sitting room/study, the eye is immediately drawn to the fine classical portrait behind the Frost-designed desk. The picture — in such a position, the classic symbol of authority — is hung in an alcove which is itself framed by pilasters and lends a touch of grandeur to the desk without dominating it. Speakers belonging to a music system are utilized to support two graceful white obelisks.

▲ This living room shows Frost's penchant for mixing exotic, Western and even classical styles. The striking work on the wall is a piece of tribal fabric from the Ivory Coast. Painted in charcoal on hand-woven strips of joined cloth, it has been attached to a piece of wool fixed to a stretcher, in an unusual combination of two very different textures.

▲
Derek Frost's furniture makes a statement, as with this vibrant console table supporting a high-strutting horse, and the picture set above it as on a plinth — a pencil drawing by Ian Brice which holds its own in spite of its monochrome tones. Two other pictures lean against the wall in languid gallery style, indicating that no art display is permanent.

Top right In the parquet-floored hall, the gently spiralled staircase is its own work of art. Its simplicity is complemented by two crumpled fabric designs by Leslie Foster which are held in glass without frames and arranged to maintain the verticality of the stairs.

► Outside the conservatory ►
are two more pictures which are perfectly paired but do not match: Ian Brice's lithograph and Suzanne Fletcher's drawing on brown paper form a kind of triptych with the main visual display created by the conservatory itself.

A country cottage, or any other type of home built in a rural tradition, usually demands an informal approach to picture arrangement – and, indeed, to all other aspects of interior design. This principle is fully endorsed by designer Liz Macfarlane, whose work encompasses a broad spectrum of skills from book illustration to package design. Her country home, shown on these pages, has evolved organically to acquire its current collection of objects and pictures. The arrangements may at first seem

somewhat haphazard – here a picture tilted slightly out of alignment, there, one overlapping the timber struts that divide some of the walls into panels. However, beneath this informality is a careful consideration of tone, shape and colour. What may seem a jumble of unpremeditated patterns and shapes in fact stems from an unerring sense of what will work where.

The colours and tones of the cottage are dictated by the rich mellow woodwork and, in the kitchen, by a beautiful wall of old brick-

work. Accordingly, the designer has chosen pictures filled with warm tones – reds, browns, earth colours – many of them framed in old frames of natural wood or rich gold. The subjects have appropriately rural overtones – traditional still lifes of fruit in the kitchen, and flower paintings in the bedrooms. Each room is distinctive, yet harmonizes perfectly with the others to create a consistent mood of rural warmth.

More of Liz Macfarlane's designs appear on pages 116; 117 (bottom left); 128; 130; 131 (left); 137.

◀ The floral theme in this bedroom, set by the paintings and wall-mounted fans, is reiterated in the fabrics on and around the bed. The Indian shawl used as a canopy makes an attractive surround to the symmetrical group of two identical fans flanking a flower painting in a weighty gold frame. (Both this flower painting and the one to the right are by the designer.)

▲
A casual display of pictures animates this welcoming kitchen. Among fruit still lifes (two of which seem to have been stacked together almost by accident) are a hunting picture and a cat hanging nonchalantly from a peg. The blue and white fruit bowl has an echo in the black-framed picture. (The cat and the smaller fruit bowl paintings are the work of the designer.)

Top right The black-painted wooden uprights on the walls of the living room help to contain the pictures without imposing too formal a grid. Across the wall a piece of furniture or a picture has been allocated to every panel, and the butterfly case has also been used as a shelf for a group of small objects. ▶

A pale seaside picture by Margaret Maitland Howard, centrally positioned beneath the decorated beam, dominates this corner of the sitting room, setting a nautical note for objects below. The small table lights are carefully placed to connect the outer edges of the painting to the chest. ▶

In the hall, the eye is
drawn to the blue sky of
the landscape: around it
are pictures remarkable
for their variety of tone.
▼

Decorative watercolours of ▶
Taj Mahal floor designs
within a single mount and
frame are set off by a
luxurious wall covering.

There is a neo-rococo airiness about the work of interior designer Nina Campbell that makes her strong use of colour all the more effective by contrast. Although her designs consciously evoke a lost age of balls, visiting cards and liveried servants, there are bold modern touches that temper the nostalgia and challenge our preconceptions. Nowhere are the paradoxes of her style shown more tellingly than in her London home.

Her picture arrangements incline towards formal symmetry. However, such displays can provide a framework for surprisingly dynamic effects, as shown by her daughter's bedroom (right) and the hall grouping (far left), where monochrome and other subdued works cluster around two landscapes in rich colour.

More of Nina Campbell's interiors can be seen on pages 19 (right); 23 (bottom); 25 (top right); 32 (top); 33 (centre left and centre bottom); 126 (right); 131 (top and right); 141; 145; 149 (left).

◄ Octagonal prints in octagonal mounts and frames form a symmetrical group, with a diagonal, leading via an informal table arrangement to a flower watercolour at floor level waiting to find a place on the wall. The unusual stick screen gives another dimension to the ensemble.

Above a bedroom table and ► chair, botanical prints in elaborate decorative mounts centre on a comic image whose thematic isolation is signalled by a plain grey surround. The diagonal network of the wallpaper pulls the group firmly together.

MEILLERS

some homes a thoroughly modern heart beats within a historic skeleton, the structure and contents forming a rich counterpoint. This is the kind of juxtaposition relished by art collector and exhibition organizer Daniel Meiller and his wife Claude, whose country home in Burgundy dates back to the 17th century.

The house contains a large modern picture collection within a classical setting. The ornate fireplaces, complementary in mood with reproduction antique statues, contrast with vibrantly modern paintings and lithographs.

Also illustrated here (right) is the Meillers' Paris apartment: as in the Burgundy home, black and white mottled bookbinding paper forms an aptly theatrical background for dramatic works of art.

◀ In the Meillers' town apartment, modern chairs balance two paintings by Bram van Velde. The column sounds a classical note.

In this bedroom a worn stone floor, mottled walls and lithographs by Bram van Velde combine to create a soothing effect. ▶

▼ *Bottom left* This vivid painting is placed to one side of the fireplace instead of in the more predictable overmantel role filled by the mirror.

▼ An abstract by Jean Messagier, lit from below, reflects the colours of the furniture.

JANE CHURCHILL

Jane Churchill is an interior designer whose style represents a new mood in traditional decoration. The basic elements she uses – including furniture and pictures with an 18th- and 19th-century feel – unmistakably borrow from the past. Yet the overall stamp is decidedly that of someone based firmly in the 20th century. There is a modern freshness and lightness of touch that make weighty things look airy and fragile things important.

This designer is essentially a modern miniaturist, as demonstrated by these views of her own home. In every room and every passage there are small-scale groupings – some of pictures alone, some of pictures combined with objects. Such ensembles are filled with detail – as with a doll's house, we are encouraged to narrow our focus and explore intently with the eye.

Decorative prints, especially botanical prints presented in sets, play a major role in this house, and full use is made of suitably ornamental mounts and frames. Additional impact is made by vases of fresh flowers everywhere which pick up the botanical theme.

The pictures and objects are tied together by the choice of soft, warm backgrounds.

Another of Jane Churchill's designs appears on page 105.

In this composition the predominant note is the warm yellow, introduced in the wallpaper and returning in some of the prints as well as in the flowers placed on the table to complete the display. The pierced blue-and-white china and imitation bamboo frames are a personal touch.

◀ Although many different
elements form this group,
nothing jars or seems
excessive. The eye is lifted
from the lyre mirror to the
flower picture and trio of
shells crowning the
display. The miniatures on
either side of the lyre
deliberately break the
symmetry.

▲
The bathroom has been
treated as a modern
printroom, in which the
prints and paper swags,
ribbons and linking chains
have been applied directly
to the wall and varnished
over to give protection from
steam. A large mirror
above the bath (not shown)
doubles the impact.

In the library of ▶
Mario Buatta's apartment,
pistachio green and white
panelled walls set off his
collection of dog portraits —
mostly spaniels — which
range in date from the late
18th century to the
Victorian era. The larger-
than-usual bows adapt and
exaggerate a historic
convention. The furniture
is bulky enough to balance
the visual weight of the
paintings. Paintings hung
over the books themselves
are a novel touch.

An eyecatching treatment, ▶
with sashes and a
porcelain ornament
offsetting the low centre of
gravity, gives emphasis to
this drawing room seating
area. An 18th-century
Italian still life with birds
and dogs is flanked by two
oval Chinese export
paintings on silvered glass.

Although America's leading exponent of the English Country House Style of interior design, Mario Buatta injects this approach with elements of wit and exaggeration that are distinctively American.

His own apartment (below and left) is part of a grand Neo-Georgian mansion on one of New York's most pleasant residential streets. The walls are glazed in subtle sunny colours. Pictures are hung from silk taffeta sashes ornamented with bows and rosettes – details which have become one of the designer's signatures. Not only do these flourishes add a decorative touch, but they also lift the eye, making a virtue of the high ceilings. As with the interiors that Buatta designs for his clients, the overall effect of the design is one of approachable grandeur.

Pictures are grouped in clusters or rows. Subjects may or may not be closely related, but frames are freely mixed: Buatta feels that they must not match unless the pictures are part of a set. He has clearly stated his rules regarding positioning: "Pictures are to be hung no less than four and no more than ten inches over the top of a piece of furniture – though in the next tier they may be as high as you like to keep balance in the room."

The charm of Mario Buatta's style, coupled with his understanding of how to show older pictures in a new and sympathetic light, makes his designs hard to resist.

This *trompe l'oeil* detail designed by Buatta for a country house in Connecticut shows his predilection for witty variations on the sash theme. Only the curtains are what they appear.
▼

THE
FRAMER'S
PORTFOLIO

The choice of mounts and frames now available is wider than ever before, with styles suitable for pictures in all sizes and media. The following pages constitute a visual "catalogue" of styles, materials and finishes, showing a range of options that cover the whole spectrum – from minimalist metal to the rococo luxury of gilded wood.

Even if you choose a relatively subdued approach to picture display, with simple frames and quietly elegant mounts, there is a vast range of permutations available. Here are some attractive possibilities for a small watercolour, print or simple decorative detail. Washlines and ink lines can be used to add distinction to the image.

BON TON.

"Look upon Lady Caroline, You appear a
"divinity!— by Jove these looks are of the première
"qualité — did love,—which those."

"On my truth Sir William You are a quiz Men

Mounts are most often seen as purely decorative but they also have an important practical function. Works on paper, whether watercolours, pastels, prints or photographs, can be damaged by condensation if left in direct contact with the glass of the frame. The cut-out or window mount creates a gap, often very fine, between the picture and the glass which prevents the picture from being spoiled.

Beyond this functional purpose mounts offer an enormous range of aesthetic possibilities: you can adjust the size of the opening so as to show more or less of the image, or use the size of the mount itself to enhance the picture – for example, to give prominence to a small work.

You must also consider texture and colour. There is a wide variety of ready-made mount cards available, in an enormous range of colours and interesting textures, including cards faced in lined or flecked papers or fabric. If these do not give the effect you want, plain card can be covered in good-quality papers such as Canson, Ingres or Fabriano. A further option is provided by handmade Japanese papers which have a more interesting texture and possess a range of colours entirely different from those of European papers. Mounts can also be covered in fabrics such as silk, cotton or linen, either plain, or patterned if a more dramatic effect is sought.

The choice of decorative finishes for mounts is also endless, ranging from simple, elegant lines of colour achieved by painting or drawing watercolour washline borders, to mounts entirely painted in watercolour or gouache. Fine strips of gold or silver paper or bands of marbled and other decorative papers can also be used, either alone or in conjunction with lines and washes (see pages 54–5).

With pictures of any worth the quality of the mount card is very important. Until a few years ago all mount card was made out of untreated wood pulp. This contains high proportions of acid and other impurities which seep out over a period of three to four years and cause progressive damage and discoloration to the picture. If you are framing an inexpensive reproduction or poster this is unlikely to matter but where the picture has any value at all, whether commercial or sentimental, it is essential to use acid-free card. This is made from rag or wood pulp treated to remove the chemicals that harm paper. It is now available in a number of colours and can of course be covered with papers or fabrics if a special tone or effect is sought.

There are more types of mounts than you might at first imagine. This selection shows how the breadth and position of wash lines, perhaps combined with other decorative treatments such as sponging, can be varied to create a wide range of styles and moods. 1. Subtle mauve and grey stipple-washed mount. 2. Pale pink washed mount with narrow washed band of stronger pink and clear inner edge outlined in gold ink. 3. Mount with a wash line containing three narrow bands of colour. 4. Pale green wash with a fine wash line in lighter green, and grey and yellow wash lines near the window. 5. Simple pink-sponged mount with a gold edge . 6. Overall pink wash with a stronger inner pink wash line. 7. Pale mount sponged in yellow and grey with fine grey line near the inner edge. 8. Pale yellow wash with inner wash line of yellow edged with orange and an outer line of fine gold. 9. Grey mount with pink and grey sponged wash line edged with pink and grey ink lines. 10. Cream mount with yellow sponged wash line and five ink lines in strong colours. 11. Pale mauve sponged wash with gold fidgeted over the top. 12. Mint green washed mount with a pale narrow inner wash line. ▶

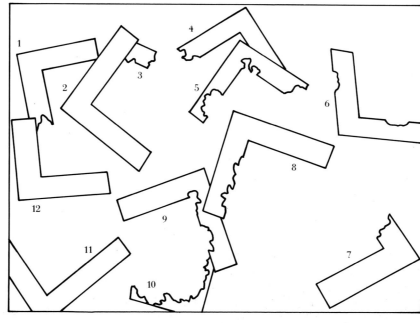

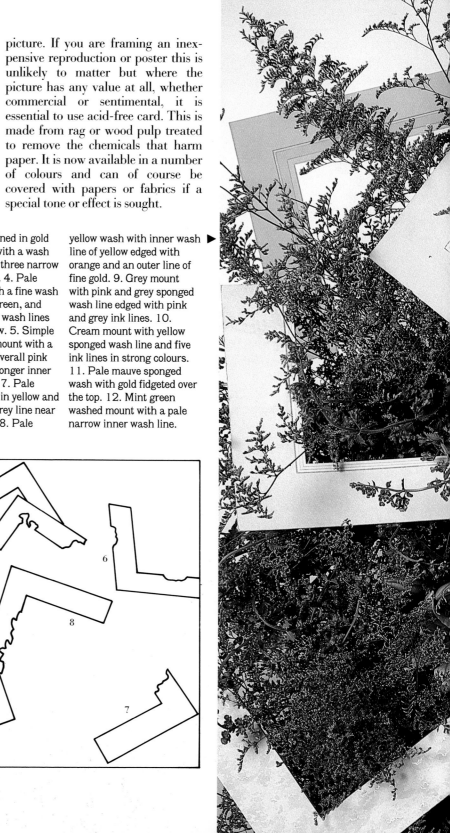

For a bold, intricate picture a plain mount to provide a breathing space between picture and frame may be all that is needed. But more often this can look bland or uninteresting and most mounts – and the pictures they surround – benefit from some form of decoration either to relieve the monotony of a plain expanse, or to subtly link the mount to its picture and frame.

The most common decorative treatment for a mount is the wash – a light application of watercolour over a water base. The washed area can then be outlined or embellished with ink lines or narrow strips of decorative paper. Lines and washes became popular in Europe toward the end of the 18th century and were well established by the 19th century. Even today they are still regarded as a simple and appropriate finish for many mounts. It is also an extremely versatile finish: the width of the washed band can be varied, as can the number of lines, the distance between them and, of course, the depth and strength of colour.

To decorate a wash line, the area or band to be coloured is treated with a light application of water; this gives an even, translucent quality to the watercolour which is applied over it. Several layers of the watercolour, or wash, are applied until a colour of the right strength is obtained. A band washed in this way can then be outlined with a pen line in a stronger shade of the same

or a contrasting colour, or in gold or silver. Next, two, three or even four other pen lines may be added in toning and contrasting shades until the desired degree of definition has been reached.

A thin line of patterned or specialist paper in fine gold is a good alternative to ink lines, and can also be used as a further decorative touch around the inner edge of the mount. This is especially effective when used to echo a gilded frame.

You can also experiment with other eye-catching techniques such as stippling, sponging or ragging over a suitable base colour. Ink lines can be added to form another design over the mount. Several shades can be used, often as many as five or six. If the picture warrants it these lines can even be extended to the edges of the mount, making squares of the corners in a final decorative flourish.

Marbelized and hand-printed papers, bought from a specialist paper shop, can look very good used as a narrow strip bordering the window of the mount. Remember, though, that a thin band is all you need, smaller even than you might at first imagine, as a wide strip will be too obvious and may destroy the impact of the image. Such papers can also be used as a background for a small print. The print is laid over a piece of the decorative paper and the mount is then cut larger than the picture to reveal a faint glimmer of the paper around the edges of the image.

▲
Dried autumn leaves on a paint-spattered background are contained within a thick mount, paint-spattered in red and brown autumnal tones and finished with a russet-red bevel.

These prettily decorated mounts are all suitable for prints whose main impact is decorative rather than seriously artistic. *Top left:* wide mount sponged all over in peach pink, and spattered with gold at the inner edge. *Top right:* outer wash of pinky-beige over a cream base, separ-

ated by a fine ink line ▶ from a narrow yellow wash. *Bottom left:* white mount with a pink and grey sponged wash line, highlighted with fine grey ink lines and a lilac-tinted bevel. *Bottom right:* speckled cream mount with terracotta and gold ink lines and a gold bevel.

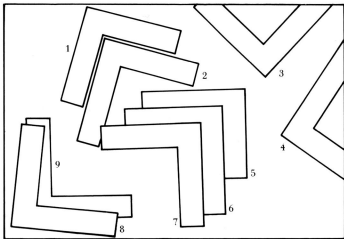

Watercolours (which are soft virtually by definition), hand-coloured decorative prints, light-toned etchings and lithographs and other media that depend on subtlety rather than instant impact, all call for delicate treatment.

Cream and off-white mounting boards are conventionally used for these types of pictures. However, pale pinks, blues, yellows and greens surrounded by a simple gold frame or pale polished wood are equally effective and more original.

Choosing the colour for the mount, of course, is just the beginning of the process. Lines, washes and other decorative devices such as stippling, sponging or ragging (see pages 54-5) will strengthen the appeal of pale mounts, which might otherwise look too reticent.

You can afford to be a little more adventurous in your choice of colour and finish for a decorative print. For example, a botanical flower print need not be mounted in an ivory-coloured mount, but perhaps in one of the more unusual colours to be found within the petals or stem.

An overall medium-weight effect can be achieved by using a double mount: a thin inner mount of a fairly bright colour offset by an outer mount in more subdued tones.

Coloured papers and papers with visible fibres or an underlying self-pattern or texture, such as marbled papers, can provide decorative interest for a busy picture without destroying its impact. They are also useful backgrounds for prints which are very small or which have a deckle (uneven) edge.

◀ Pale mounts for subtle pictures need not be plain, as shown by these mounts classically decorated in muted colours. 1. Cream mount with broad ochre wash line, edged with green lines. 2. Cream mount with azure wash line and sepia outer lines. 3. Cream mount with fine strip of gold paper edged with sepia lines. 4. White mount with narrow and wide sky blue wash lines edged with sepia and ochre ink lines. 5. Cream mount with blue wash line, thin strip of gold paper and outer grey-blue lines. 6. Cream mount with pink wash line, sepia outer line and inner gold band. 7. Cream mount with yellow wash line, a thin strip of gold paper and sepia outer lines. 8. Cream mount with pale green wash line edged with blue-grey lines. 9. Cream mount with burnt sienna wash line and light blue outer lines.

BOLD MOUNTS

Images executed in heavy tones or strong rich colours – for example, architectural prints, maps, gouaches, and Indian or Oriental pictures – may need mounts that have been washed over in far stronger colours than is usual for paler pictures in order to contain and balance the strong image.

Strength of colour in the mount is achieved by building up the layers of wash (see page 54), repeating the colour a number of times. An alternative is to use gouache. This is a type of watercolour paint made with a white pigment base with the result that it is opaque and thus denser than pure watercolour.

Marbelized and hand-printed papers can look very good as decorative embellishments on strong-coloured mounts. A wide strip may be too obvious and steal attention away from the picture, so restrict yourself to a thin surround: about ¾in (2 cm) or less will usually be suitable.

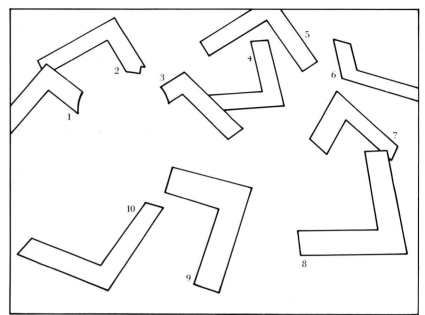

◀ A selection of bold mounts for accentuating strong pictures, such as bold monochrome architectural prints. 1. Pink dragged mount with clear inner edge, and a gold band. 2. Sand brown mount with a wide grey-beige wash line, edged with a strong black line; toward the inner edge, a gold band and deeper sand inner wash line. 3. Green-washed mount with a strong, narrow band of moss green and an inner wash of peppermint carried over to the bevel. 4. Grey mount with band of prussian blue and ochre marbled paper, with gold and ochre lines. 5. Beige-washed mount with band of pink and gold spattered marbled paper edged with fine ink lines, and a gold bevel. 6. Broad beige wash over cream base with an inner blue-grey wash line bordered by a band of antiqued grey and brown marbled paper and a gold paper strip. 7. Cream mount with a broad light sepia wash line, narrow inner wash line in heavy sepia and antiqued gold paper border. 8. Cream mount with strong blue dragging over the outer section and on the inner section a cream wash line edged with a gold line and fine ink lines. 9. Broad band of sponged grey-green wash with a strong sepia edge and an inner wash line in blue edged with sepia and a gold band. 10. Beige mount with a broad brown wash line, strong brown inner wash line and an antiqued gold band.

Multiple mounts are made from two or more individual mounts cut in "steps", one mount sitting over another so that only a part of the lower mount, sometimes very little, is revealed.

The simplest multiple mount consists of a light inner mount and a dark outer mount cut so as to show only a narrow fillet of the lighter card. This is useful as a device to add depth and perspective to the mount. It can also be particularly effective in mounting pastels. The colours of pastel drawings often need a mount in a mid-tone. On its own this could look drab but a light inner mount counteracts this effect. In addition, the double mount gives an added distance between the glass and the artwork, essential with lightly fixed pastels, charcoals and chalks (see pages 22-3).

Multiple mounts also offer a number of decorative possibilities: if the mount is cut so as to show a wider piece of the inner mount, ¾-1in (2-3cm), the area can be embellished with a narrow wash line or a strip of gold or marbelized paper.

An interesting effect can also be achieved by sticking a sheet of Japanese or other good quality coloured paper onto a previously cut mount card so that it wraps over the bevel.

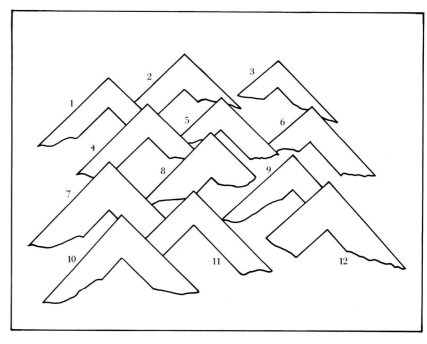

◀ Double and triple mounts work particularly well if you exploit the opportunities for vivid contrasts — smooth against rough, plain against pattern, dark against light and so on. 1. Simple double mount of cream and grey-brown. 2. Cream inner mount with band of sepia-edged gold, surrounded by chalky-blue outer mount. 3. Gold-wrapped inner mount sets off outer mount wrapped in blue-grey Japanese paper. 4. Outer mount wrapped in steely-blue Japanese paper, enlivened by inner mount wrapped in gold and edged with pink marbled paper. 5. Purple-brown Ingres paper wrapped around outer mount with strongly antiqued gold paper wrapped around the inner. 6. Triple mount with the outer wrapped in strong blue Japanese paper, the centre in deep red and the inner — a mount of double thickness — in gold paper. 7. Outer mount of ginger brown blends with inner mount of cream, finished with pink wash line. 8. Dark outer mount juxtaposed with decorative inner cream mount, with sponged wash line of sepia, yellow and grey, defined by fine gold band edged with sepia and grey. 9. Rich russet Japanese paper wrapped around the outer mount; the inner is wrapped in silver paper and antiqued with sepia. 10. Outer mount wrapped in grey Japanese paper, the inner in a strip of blue and brown marbled paper with a wrapped gold bevel. 11. Dark plum and coral Japanese papers wrapped around inner and outer mounts. 12. Prussian blue outer mount with a gold band and inner mount with strip of blue and purple marbled paper and a yellow wash line.

Fabric can be used to cover both mounts and slips. There is a wide range of textures available, from raw silk to hand-woven linens, that can be used to surround and enliven an image.

A common application of fabrics in the early part of this century was in covering a slip frame with linen or canvas for an oil painting. Although this idea is somewhat dated, fabric is now widely used as an alternative medium to a painted card mount; either because it is hard to find a mount of the right colour, or because the depth or texture of fabric would be more appropriate to the artwork being displayed. Remember, however, that even a lightweight material, unless carefully chosen to suit the artwork, can overwhelm a delicate watercolour or fine etching.

Choose natural fabrics wherever possible as these are easier to handle and glue than artificial fibres, and tend to look better.

You can use fabric to tie in a picture with the decorative scheme of a room. This is not to suggest that if the room is a bower of flowered chintz the mounts for the prints should be the same riot of bloom. A plain colour of fabric, perhaps one of the colours used in the background of the main scheme, would be the best choice, or a small geometric print, so long as the colours are fairly subdued and the pattern is scaled to complement the picture. This is an area for experimentation. Unlikely-seeming patterns – flower buds and gold stamped prints – could be effective if chosen judiciously. If you have fabric-covered walls, do not use exactly the same fabric for the mount, as this will cause the picture to merge with its background.

Hessian was often used for mounting pictures in the 1940s and 50s, but it can look a bit drab with newer works. However, if you are framing a picture of that period, particularly a collage or similar work, hessian is still an appropriate way to keep the display in period.

Velvet is an interesting fabric to use on a mount. Unfortunately man-made velour in imitation of velvet is traditionally used on ready-made frames and has itself a reputation for tawd Choose real cotton or silk velvet instead, which is warm and subtle.

Fabric is an ideal lining in box frames made to display objects: if you are framing a fan, for example, use a fine fabric. Silk is best of all but it is best to avoid very thin silk as the glue marks are likely to show through the weave. Silk is also a better option than velvet for any collections of small, light objects such as butterflies and beetles, as velvet collects and shows dust, which can give collections set on velvet a rather desolate air.

If you do choose to use silk or velvet always glaze the box or frame containing the artwork to stop dust and dirt getting in. Linen, which is less delicate, would also be suitable for an open frame or box display.

The strong shapes and motifs of medals can look very striking against the bright, flat colours of felt. Do not use felt with pictures on paper, as it is acidic and will eventually destroy the artwork.

◀ Fabric of almost any colour and pattern can be used to enliven a plain mount or slip. 1. Flat mount covered in pale *ikat* weave cotton with a grey and yellow pattern. 2. Blue slubbed cotton weave on wide, flat mount. 3. Flat mount covered with pinky-beige cotton moiré weave. 4. Chinese natural shantung silk on a flat mount. 5. Check madras cotton used diagonally on a bevelled slip. 6. Slip clad in blue and yellow poplin shirting with the stripes running transversely. 7. Traditional black and cream mattress ticking with the stripes running longitudinally along a flat slip. 8. Slip wrapped in saxe-blue and white ticking. 9. Terracotta and cream ticking with stripes running diagonally across a bevelled slip. 10. Heavy striped cream herringbone weave cotton on a concave slip with inner edge. 11. Lightweight natural linen on a narrow slip. 12. Lightweight natural Irish linen on a thin flat mount. 13. Glazed peach cotton on a flat mount. 14. Fine Indian straw-coloured cotton on a flat mount.

INTRODUCING FRAMES

A t its simplest a frame is four pieces of wood moulding joined together. Moulding – the strip of wood from which the outer edges of the frame are made – comes in a range of lengths and widths and in a wide variety of decorative styles.

Framer's mouldings are specifically designed for making picture frames and the only type you are likely to find at the framer's. (Builder's moulding, used, for example, to bead and trim doors, cupboards and skirting boards, is not usually suitable for framing, as it has no rabbet (rebate) – the stepped edged that allows the mount, picture and glass to sit neatly in place.)

Although mouldings can be finished by hand, the most common sort is machine-made and encompasses every style and type of decoration. The finish is applied to 6 or 8 feet (180 or 245cm) lengths in a factory rather than by the framer himself. The wood can be plain, stained and varnished, painted and lacquered, or finished in gold or silver. There are mouldings made in the manner of period frames, with plaster work formed into classical patterns, and stepped frames with ribbed or trellised designs.

Almost any shape frame can be found: there is the perfectly flat frame suitable for covering with fabric or a decorative paint finish; the reverse frame where the moulding slopes away from the picture; and concave and convex frames. Some concave frames are known as spoon, scoop or hollow frames because they look as if they have been scooped out in the centre. Another traditional style of frame is built in steps and known as a window frame. Painters such as Whistler and Hogarth have given their names to other shapes that have entered the standard repertoire. Some frame names recall particular places and cultures – for example, Flemish and Florentine.

In addition to these standard forms, there are other, less usual types of frame for framing needs. For example, you might use a floating frame for a modern oil painting (see page 165), a box frame for displaying special objects (see page 32) or a double-glass frame for a manuscript (see page 159).

The choices of wood for a frame are many. Maple, walnut, ash, mahogany ramin, pine, oak – each has its own characteristic colour and texture that makes it suitable for a particular type of picture. Wood is a versatile material that can be finished in a large number of ways. It can be left plain to show the grain, and sealed and polished; or stained in any number of shades – realistic or fanciful. Gesso can be applied to form a smooth luminous base for gilding and decoration. Alternatively, the wood can be painted or veneered. The veneer can be plain or finished in marquetry, applied in strips to form a pattern. Decorative paint finishes, fashionable on walls and furniture, work remarkably well on frames too.

Different mouldings and finishes can be combined for decorative effect – for example, a narrow veneered wood frame could be used inside a gold moulding as a slip. Canvas-covered slips can also be used to provide a contrast of colour and texture.

Of course, not every picture needs a frame made from wood: there are various other options. Metal frames, often used for photographs, posters and modern abstracts, usually take the form of extruded aluminium, brass, or steel, and come in a wide variety of colours.

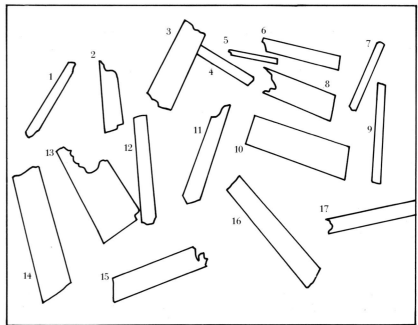

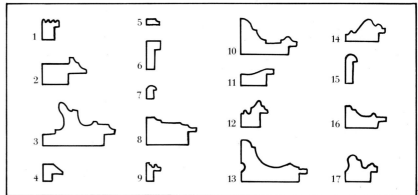

A selection of traditional and modern mouldings. 1. Ribbed moulding, used alone or with slips. 2. Wide-lipped flat moulding, used alone or as a slip. 3. Swept moulding, the base for many classic gilded frames. 4. Bevelled slip, can be gessoed, painted or fabric-covered. 5. Small flat slip. 6. Flat moulding. Useful as an outer covering for a box frame. 7. Bead moulding for prints or drawings. 8. Wide window moulding for oils and large works on paper. 9. Small spoon moulding for prints and small works. 10. Concave moulding for oils. 11. Classic shallow reverse moulding used as a base for decorative finishes and veneers. 12. Gothic frame for etchings and other prints. 13. Large modern concave spoon moulding, mainly for oils. 14. Large reverse convex moulding, similar in shape to builder's moulding. 15. Hockey stick moulding, used plain or finished. 16. Spoon moulding for works with perspective. 17. Small hollow moulding for watercolours.

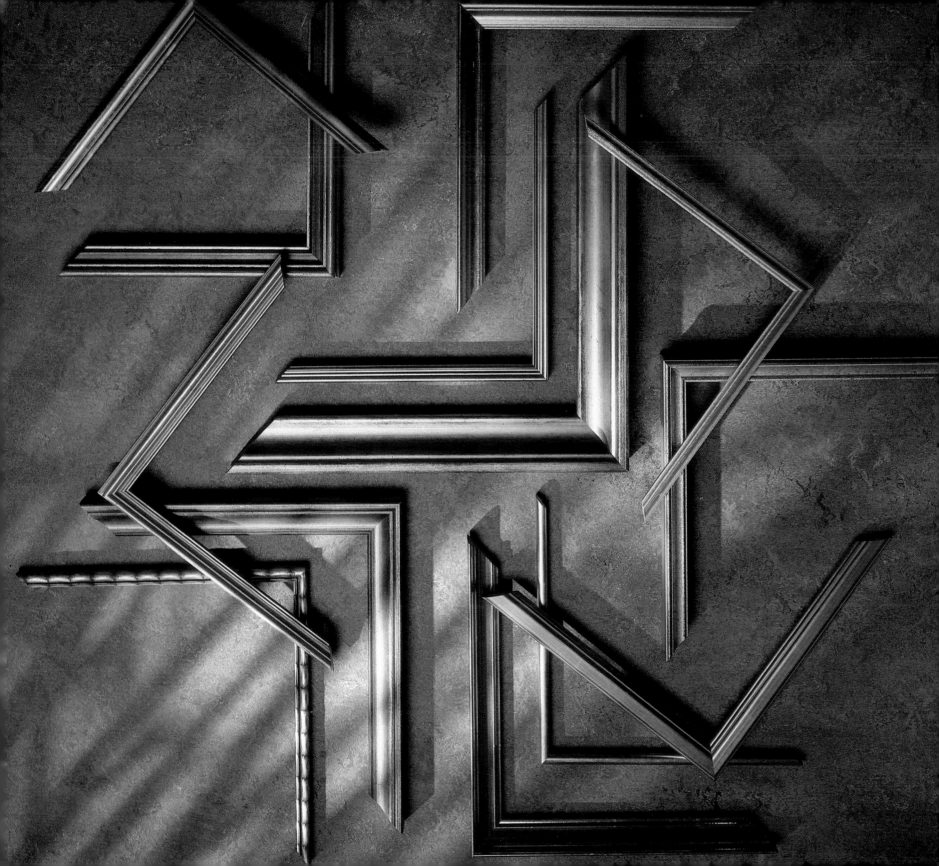

◀ This group of individual and attractive frames shows that manufactured mouldings need not look dull or mass-produced. 1. Good-quality metal leaf applied over a painted ground to simulate gilded bole. 2. Frame with two base coats of yellow and green, with gold applied over the top then rubbed back to reveal the colours. 3. Spoon frame with bright gold finish. 4. Reverse moulding coloured orange-gold over a red base. 5. Yellow gold applied over a brown base, distressed and then spattered black. 6. Almost flat moulding with imitation gold leaf applied in sections, then lightly distressed. 7. Brightly-coloured gold bead frame. 8. Frame for architectural prints, with gold applied to inner and outer edges and the centre coloured black. 9. Spoon frame with green-gold finish, distressed over a reddish ground. 10. Free imitation of bamboo, with bright gold applied over red ground. 11. Classic moulding for watercolours, with yellow-gold finish, spattered grey. 12. Frame with bright metallic finish, suitable for prints. 13. Spoon frame for oil paintings, with gold over a red-brown base.

Gold frames are of two kinds. There are those made up from mouldings supplied ready-finished in gold leaf or gold-coloured paint; and those assembled from lengths of raw wood moulding and then finished in gold leaf by the framer. The second type involves lengthy preparation by hand and is considerably more expensive than the first.

Commercially available gold mouldings come in a vast range of shapes and finishes. At one end of the scale are flat or half-round shapes surfaced with clear bright gold: these are often suitable for modern works and for simple subjects. Earlier works – antique prints, or 18th- and 19th-century watercolours and the like – generally demand a frame with a wider moulding and, preferably, some additional toning or antiquing of the metal finish to give an impression of age. The gold finish itself can vary from a neutral yellow to a greenish or reddish tint: your eye will be the only true guide as to which is going to look best with your picture.

The gold finish is often applied over a coloured undercoat, usually reddish brown, and is rubbed away slightly to reveal some of the base coat beneath. This treatment is intended to imitate the look of an old gold-leaf frame. Also available are gold frames with a semi-transparent layer of colour applied over the top.

Gold-leaf frames have a depth of colour that is lacking in frames made up of mass-produced mouldings treated as described above. Moreover, they retain their looks, whereas mass-produced gold may eventually turn dull and discoloured.

Gold leaf is indeed real gold that has been hammered into extremely thin sheets – so thin that if a breeze catches them they can disintegrate. It is sold in books of leaves, about 3in (7.5cm) square, with tissue packed between each leaf. It cannot be applied directly to a raw wood frame, as it needs a porous substance to which it can adhere. The frames are therefore prepared with several coats of gesso – chalk whiting mixed with size – creating a suitable base which is then sandpapered to a smooth finish. Then three or four coats of bole are applied in syrup form on top of the gesso. It is the bole, which comes in shades of red, yellow, black, brown or blue, that gives colour to the gold when the frame is "distressed" – that is, when the gold is rubbed down so that the base colour shows through.

The gold leaf is applied in overlapping sheets. Thus, if the gold leaf is rubbed down – to distress it – a thicker layer is left where the sheets overlap. This gives the distinctive ridging often seen on gold-leaf frames.

The gold leaf itself also comes in different tints – from the classic yellow-gold to golds with reddish or greenish tones – each imparting its own distinctive mood. Red creates the warmest effect; yellow, the most usual colour for gilding, is more neutral.

The gold can be left matt but more usually it is burnished – that is, polished with an agate burnisher to produce a bright, shiny finish. If you want a deep gold effect with no toning, the framer will probably need to double-gild the frame, applying two layers of gold leaf and then burnishing without distressing.

Gold leaf can also be toned after gilding, using dull tempera, water-colour washes or thin oil colours, all of which have the effect of dulling the finish to prevent it from being too obtrusive.

On generously-sized, fairly complex frames different treatments can be combined. For example, the inner and outer sections may be burnished and the centre left matt. Or parts of the frame could be left ungilded, showing either the gesso finished with a thin wash of colour, or the colour of the bole, with other parts distressed or toned.

A crucial thing to remember about gold-leaf frames is that the leaf rubs away with water. *Never wash gold leaf* – use a soft dry cloth only.

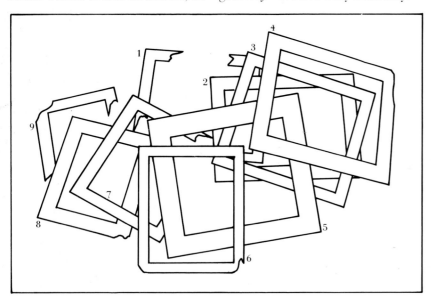

A selection of gold frames with various decorative treatments. 1. Yellow gold over red bole, distressed, with a matt finish. 2. Gold leaf over red bole on inner and outer sections, with centre area left ungilded to show the bole colour. 3. Distressed yellow gold over purple bole, strongly distressed in the centre and burnished on inner and outer sections. 4. Yellow gold over red bole, with sections alternately burnished and ungilded on a matt gold background. 5. Hollow frame of gold over red bole, with central section in dark tortoiseshell and inner section burnished. 6. Pink gold over deep pink bole, distressed and burnished. 7. Spoon frame of gold over black, lightly distressed. 8. Gold on red, laid in a diagonal "brick" pattern. 9. Distressed gold over red, left matt except where burnished at the corners. ▶

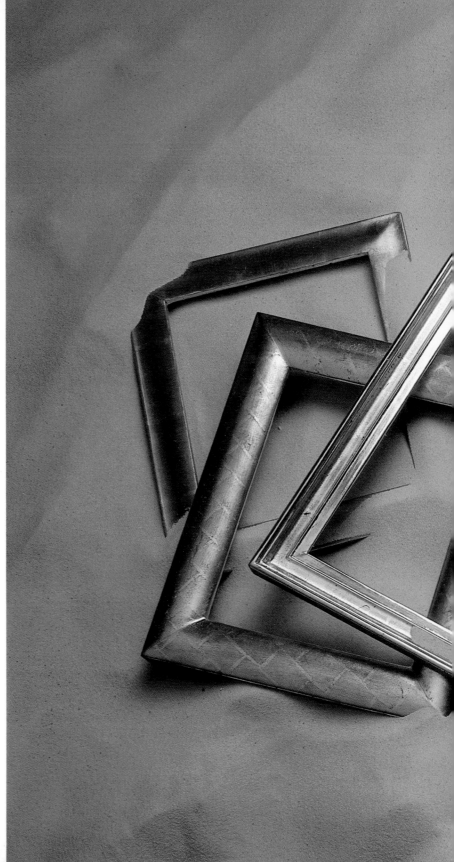

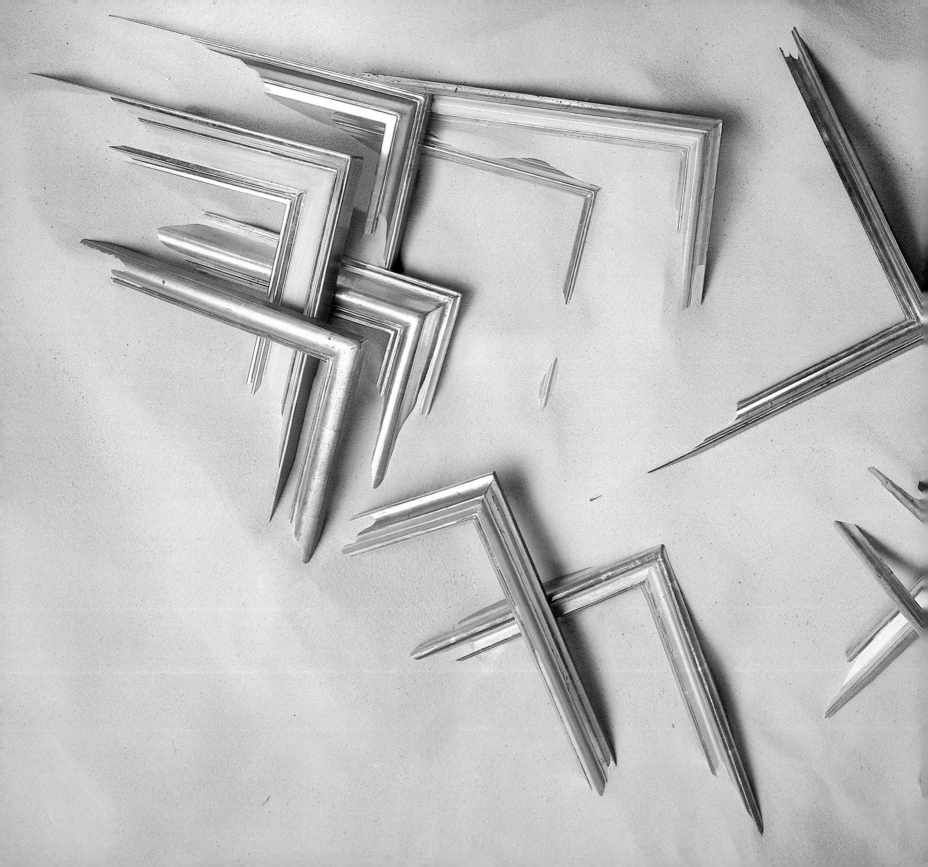

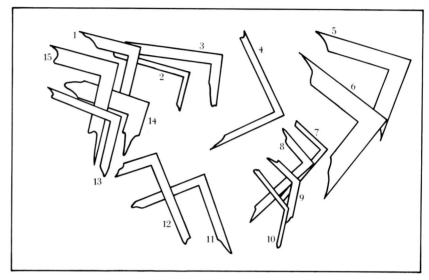

◀ Gold leaf is a versatile and sophisticated finish, whether used on a whole frame or as a decorative highlight for other finishes. 1. Spoon frame with red bole and only inner and outer sections gilded and burnished. 2. Narrow Gothic moulding, highly burnished in yellow gold. 3. Reverse moulding with inner and outer sections distressed and central sections gessoed and spattered. 4. Dark blue bole-based frame, gilded and distressed. 5. Black bole base with bright burnished gold on inner and outer sections and heavy black central section. 6. Pale gold leaf lightly distressed over blue bole, with wide blue central section. 7. Classic print frame of brightly burnished gold leaf over red bole base. 8. Distressed gold leaf, highlighted with white gessoed central strip. 9. Spoon moulding with heavily distressed gold leaf over red bole. 10. Simple cushion moulding with distressed gold leaf over red bole. 11. Distressed gold over red bole on inner and outer sections with central area finished in matt gold. 12. Reverse moulding with burnished gold on inner and outer sections and painted central section over red bole. 13. Simple, slightly rounded distressed moulding. 14. Burnished gold leaf over yellow bole, with central ochre section. 15. Wide reverse moulding finished with bright burnished gold leaf.

SILVER AND WHITE GOLD FRAMES

As with gold frames, silver frames either come in mass-produced form or are made up in raw wood and hand-finished by the framer. Here again the ready-made frames vary enormously, from brightly polished with clean, simple lines to those with complicated mouldings and toned, artificially aged finishes.

Hand-finished silver frames are made using the same techniques as gold frames. Silver leaf can be used but it has a bright metallic appearance unsuitable with most pictures. A common alternative is white gold leaf, which is an alloy of roughly equal parts of silver and 12-carat gold. The bole is normally either blue or black, but red can be used, yielding a warm effect when the frame is distressed.

All silver and white gold finishes tarnish so they are usually burnished and protected with a varnish which can be tinted. A sepia tint is usually used as it dulls bright surfaces and creates an impression of age.

Silver frames are often a good choice for pencil and charcoal drawings; also for modern work with strong colours, particularly reds and blues. Although seldom appropriate for works of the 19th century and earlier, they can look good around paintings where grey or silvery tones predominate.

Silver is also suitable for photographs, especially freestanding pictures for tables and mantelpieces. It flatters the black and white tones of old photographs. Over a small area it is less likely to compete with the picture for attention than it would if stretched to a more generous scale.

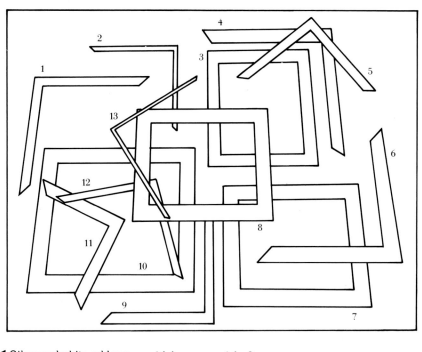

◄ Silver and white gold can be used plain or together with lacquer, coloured varnish or paint to create a modern and sophisticated effect. The combination of silver and black or grey can be particularly striking, as two of these examples demonstrate. 1. White gold leaf over red bole, distressed, with a matt finish. 2. Traditional print frame in antiqued silver, finished with yellow varnish. 3. Spoon frame in distressed white gold leaf over blue bole, with inner and outer sections burnished and the centre left matt. 4. Silver leaf over red bole, distressed, with matt centre. 5. Metallic silver, antiqued with brown varnish. 6. Silver leaf distressed over black bole, separated by a fine red line from a black lacquer border. 7. White gold leaf over grey bole with alternate matt and burnished diagonal sections. 8. Oxidized silver for a smoky effect, over red bole. 9. Imitation silver leaf over a red base. 10. White gold leaf over black bole, with alternate sections burnished, unburnished or ungilded in a harlequin-type design. 11. Ribbed metallic silver over alternating blue and red ground. 12. Print frame in metallic silver over red, with grey antiquing. 13. Narrow bright silver bead frame.

Antique frames are now recognized as an art form in themselves and should be treated as such.

If you have bought an old oil painting without a frame, first research the period in which the picture was painted in order to find out what sort of frame it had originally. If you can't find an original frame of the period you could then approach a frame-maker who specializes in making up reproduction antique frames and who will help you decide on the right style.

Of course the early decades of our own century are "period" too — certainly as far as frames go. Frames made during the 1920s were usually finished in the fashionable tones of white-grey or silver, and these finishes still look best with paintings of that period. For once in its long history, the gold frame was out of fashion.

If you have an old frame that is even partially good, don't just throw it away: look into the possibilities of restoring it — particularly if it is wooden and the decoration on it has been carved. You may find, after investing a little money in its restoration, that it is worth a considerable amount of money. This does not just apply to 18th-century or earlier frames. A Victorian plaster frame in relatively good condition is worth having restored, and fine decorated frames of the 1920s and 30s are becoming rare — particularly if they still contain the original painting.

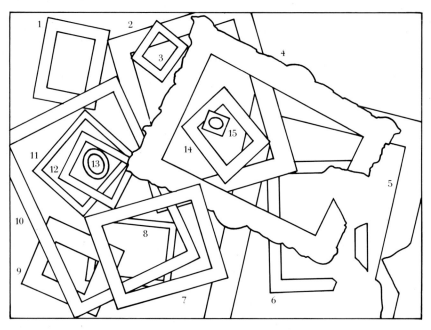

Styles of frames have been influenced by the development of decorative styles generally, from scrolled motifs of the Baroque age to the simpler lines of the Neo-classical period. 1. Ogee-shaped maple veneer frame with gilt slip. English, c. 1860. 2. French "ribbon twist" gilt frame, c. 1850. 3. Cushion-shape maple veneer frame with gilt slip. English, c. 1860. 4. 1860 copy of frame created by Jacopo Sansovino in Renaissance Italy. 5. "Pre-Raphaelite" gilded oak frame. English, c. 1870. 6. Ogee-shaped rosewood veneer frame. English, c. 1860. 7. 1860 American imitation of carved giltwood Louis XIV "Rose Corner" style frame. ▶ 8. "Biedermeier" pitch pine frame for prints and gouaches. French, c. 1870. 9. 1930 English copy of 17th-century Dutch "Ripple" frame. 10. French "Empire" frame with Neo-classical decoration with swan motif at centres and corners, c. 1810. 11. "Whistler" pattern variation watercolour frame. English, c. 1880. 12. English Regency hollow frame, c. 1820. 13. French oval miniature frame of the mid-19th century. 14. Silver gilt "Alma Tadema" style frame. English, c. 1880. 15. Pressed brass oval spandrel miniature frame. English, c. 1800.

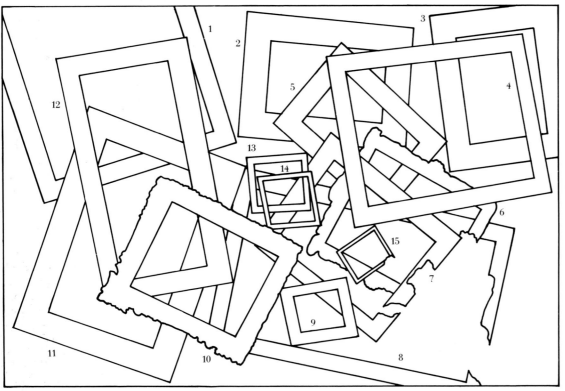

A further selection of antique and reproduction frames 1. Carved "Chippendale" giltwood frame. English c. 1760. 2. French mid-19th century frame with running acanthus leaf decoration and leaf and berry outer pattern. 3. "Barbizon School" gilt frame. French, c. 1860. 4. Modern copy of a Spanish 17th-century black frame with gilt stencil pattern at corners and centre. 5. French Neo-classical "Fluted Hollow" frame with acanthus leaf corners, c. 1850. 6. English 17th-century "Sunderland" style carved giltwood frame derived from Dutch "Lutma" frame. 7. "Lely ▶ Plaque" carved giltwood frame. English, c. 1660. 8. German "Jugendstil" carved giltwood frame, c. 1890. 9. Georgian spoon gold hollow frame. English, c. 1800. 10. Louis XIV "Rose Corner" carved gilt frame, c. 1700. 11. "Watts" gilt frame. English, 1880. 12. 19th-century copy of 16th-century Bolognese carved giltwood frame. 13. Carved "Hogarth" style black and gold frame. English, c. 1750. 14. Running water lily leaf patterned English frame, c. 1910. 15. Small, narrow German silver gilt "Barley Twist" frame, c. 1840.

Dark stained oak and pine were for many years the most popular choice for frames and furniture, but taste is moving toward lighter, natural wood finishes.

Oak, pine and ramin are all suitable and inexpensive woods. Oak, which has a pinkish tone, can be used plain or slightly stained. Or try oak which has been limed — given a thin white wash, rubbed back to show some of the natural wood.

Ramin and pine are used as the base for treatments such as dragging, sponging and spattering (see page 80) but can be used undecorated. Ramin is a fairly plain white wood with no discernible grain. When sanded and polished it has a simple elegance with bright posters and modern prints. Pine is also light and has a rather rustic feel. It is best when stained to tone down the knots which may give it an uneven quality; but its natural finish is attractive where there is other pine in the room.

Poplar is a less common, creamy-white wood which, together with sycamore, is an elegant and modern alternative to aluminium and works well in large areas.

Maple is popular but can look orange if it is of poor quality. Walnut veneer is more original and luxurious, and has recently become much easier to find. Mahogany veneer, which has replaced the once popular but less subtle mahogany stain, is another warm, rich wood.

Luxurious and elaborate inlaid wood veneers, or marquetry frames, although expensive, are enjoying a renaissance. They are especially suitable for highly decorative sporting or architectural prints.

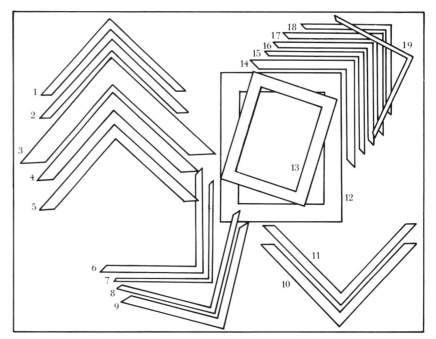

◀ Wood may be chosen not only for its warm, mellow appearance but also for its knots and graining which can be highly decorative. Expensive woods may be used as thin veneers or intricately jigsawed in a marquetry pattern. 1. Simple bevelled maple frame. 2. Rounded frame in walnut veneer. 3. Bird's eye maple frame with narrow gold inner slip. 4. Small patterned bird's eye maple frame. 5. Walnut veneer frame. 6. Dark mahogany veneer frame edged in black. 7. Bead frame stained to a cherry colour. 8. Ribbed white wood frame with ebony inlay. 9. Oak frame stained to a deeper grey-black shade. 10. Flat frame with light figured veneer. 11. Frame made from a veneer of laminated wood cut across the grain. 12. Flat walnut veneer frame with narrow fruitwood bands. 13. Figured walnut veneer with narrow inner gold slip. 14. Frame stained to imitate birchwood, with an inlaid marquetry band. 15. Chestnut stained frame with marquetry band. 16. Allover running ribbon design in marquetry. 17. Marquetry inlaid frame in star design. 18. Honey-colour stained frame with thin line of inlaid ebony. 19. Four-colour inlaid marquetry frame.

◀ *Far left* Plain solid wood may be appropriate in uncluttered modern surroundings. With the exception of the darker unstained mahogany on the right, these frames are all made from oak. The narrow ridged frame over the mahogany is limed oak, while the others are unstained but have been polished and sealed. The common but versatile profile of the two narrow frames on the left is known as Gothic.

Painted finishes on wooden frames encompass all the decorative paint effects now so popular on walls and woodwork throughout the house.

Dragging is the simplest of all painted finishes. The technique consists of a white or pale oil-based undercoat, sanded smooth and then painted with a tinted oil glaze. The glaze is swiftly pulled or dragged off with a stiff dry brush, leaving thin vertical lines.

This sort of frame works equally well on watercolours, prints and oils. On watercolours where the subject is a delicate pale scene, a frame dragged in equally delicate colours is an alternative to gold.

Sponging and spattering are the other most popular finishes. On the whole, these sorts of effects work best on a picture that is already highly decorative in itself such as a decorative print. Sponging is usually done with natural – or sea – sponges, the size of the sponge giving a different shape to the mottling. A sponged effect can be applied both positively and negatively: that is, the paint can be sponged *on* with a dabbing motion to a dry base and left to dry where it sits, or alternatively, it can be applied with a brush, and immediately dabbed *off* in parts with a sponge.

Sponging can be done in a combination of colours to give a cloudy effect, or just one colour can be sponged onto a white or cream base to create a more definite outline. Watercolour sponging onto gesso is an option for soft-toned prints. The gesso can be sealed with white shellac. This mixture acts as a luminous ivory base for the paint and prevents it from sinking into the frame. A gentler form of sponging, more akin to marbling, is to use crumpled fabric to lift off the painted colour. A mount to go with this frame could take the same tone as the sponging, but in a slightly stronger shade.

Spattering is a method by which paint is flicked with a brush onto a frame which has already been painted in one plain colour. Contrasting or darker colours are spattered onto the painted base, or even a combination of colours, the second applied after the first has dried, and so on. Or designs can be made by spattering sections only. For example, the corners can be masked off while the rest of the frame is spattered. These can be left plain or decorated with a motif to highlight the spattered effect.

Painted finishes can transform a plain wooden frame into a dramatic complement for a watercolour or decorative print. 1. Reverse frame with finely-sponged finish in coral and emerald over a yellow base. 2. Etruscan red reverse frame edged in black with sponged black sections and clear corners. 3. Shallow reverse frame dragged in pale white-grey over coral-coloured base. 4. Frame dragged in butter yellow over a grey-green base. 5. Wide dramatic reverse frame with emerald green sponged over dark bottle green, and green-black edges. 6. Shallow grey-blue reverse frame, densely spattered in black with sections left clear around the corners. 7. Shallow reverse frame with a spatter finish of black, mid-blue and spots of white over pale blue, with heavier spattering in the corners. 8. Gothic frame, with blue sponged over white, and bold violet edging. 9. Spattered green and apricot finish over an off-white base with green on the inner edge and apricot on the outer. 10. Sponged frame in mid-green over lighter green with the sponged colour repeated on the outer edge. 11. Very shallow reverse frame in orange-yellow, dragged over a gesso base. 12. Sponged Gothic frame in mid-blue over baby blue.

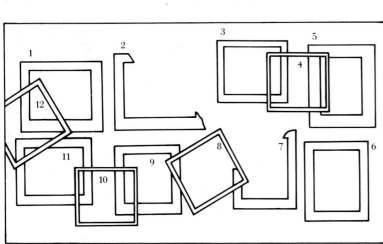

A frame with a painted design on it can look sophisticated and distinctive, but this is also one of the hardest effects to carry off well. If you have a firm hand and a sure eye you can attempt some of the easier methods, such as stencilling, yourself. However, for more complex painted designs it is best to find a framer who specializes in this field.

When commissioning a professional to paint a frame, it is not advisable to expect him or her to copy something directly from a book. Attempting to impose too rigid a brief will inhibit the look of the finished design. If you are in favour of a particular motif — perhaps one from a 19th-century book of ornament — consult the artist to see whether it can be simplified or adapted to fit the frame.

Of course, the picture itself must serve as a guideline to the type of design that will be suitable. A sinuous art nouveau print would obviously be compatible with a frame design of swaying, serpentine motifs. Scale is an important consideration. In stencilling, for example, the shape and design of the stencilled motifs should be simple, and not larger in scale than the elements within the image. Rigidly geometric designs tend to look best on a small frame; over a large area they can be overpowering.

Early medieval frames were often highly coloured as well as gilded, and motifs were painted on to accentuate the subject of the painting. Dutch painters of the 15th century often repeated images from the painting in the frame itself — even using a degree of *trompe l'oeil*. Today many serious artists insist on designing their own frames as a part of the total impact of the work.

For a naive-looking effect, the design can be painted onto the raw wood and then sealed. This approach can look impressive on a wood with a strong grain.

Primitive combed designs (in the style of the early American settlers) can be successful as frame decorations. A colour wash or a tinted glaze is applied with a brush and then combed through with a wide-toothed comb. Instead of the ochre tones that were once so popular, combed frames appear fresher in warm blues or greens, now more widely available than they once were.

A further selection of decorated frames, each one subtle and unique. 1. Coral and green stencilled design on a flat frame with an off-white base. 2. Soft-green figure-of-eight motifs highlighted in fine gold, applied to a flat frame with an off-white base. 3. Concave frame with a pale terracotta base, dragged along the inner edge, spattered, then lightly marbled on the outer edge. 4. Frame stencilled with a pale green and coral flower motif, reminiscent of early American stencil designs. 5. Flat moss-green frame with a two-tone chequerboard pattern and a coral inner edge. 6. Narrow water-green frame with red and green motifs on the corners. 7. Flat frame with emerald and coral washes floated and fidgeted on, then varnished. 8. Frame with alternate sections of grey-green and ochre marbling and blue spattering. 9. Flat frame with a gesso base and a raised edge, finished with gold leaf corners and a grecian blue motif. 10. Flat frame loosely sponged in aquamarine with an 18th-century-style freehand decoration in yellow ochre and cream. 11. Flat gessoed frame with gold leaf corners and turquoise border and lightly painted panels. 12. Tray frame with combed beige and lobster finish.

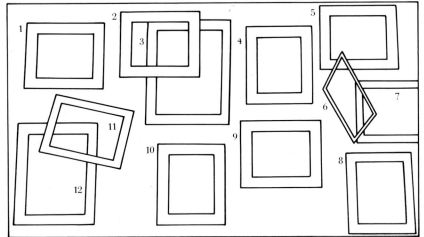

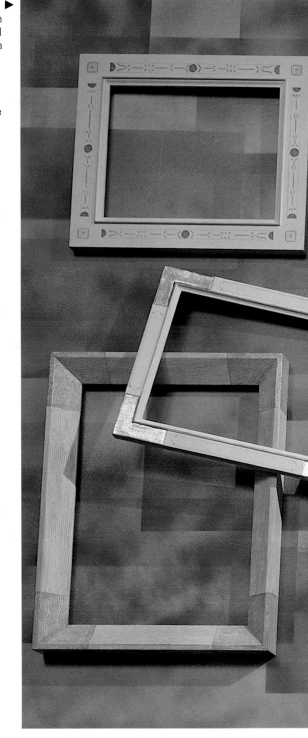

There is a wide range of fake wood effects that work well on picture frames. Indeed, many of them look almost better than real woods, whose characteristics do not always reveal themselves to best advantage within the narrow compass of a frame. Pine is a good example: with all the knots and whorls in the right place, an imitation pine frame can look superb in a sympathetic setting – and with a suitable image inside.

Faux bois (literally, "false wood") is a method of achieving a whole range of realistic imitation finishes or fanciful effects. Veins which may, but need not, resemble the real wood are painted on with a small brush. Alternatively, a glaze is applied and lines dragged through it with a comb to reveal the base colour.

Artificial graining – an art that virtually died out at the beginning of this century but is now rapidly recovering its popularity – is best applied to relatively wide frames, so that you can clearly see the effect of

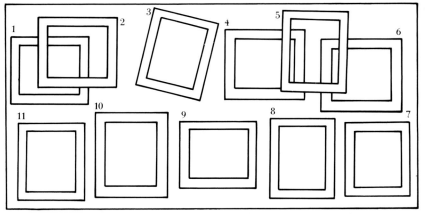

used extensively. It is now very difficult to find but its effective pale gold tones can be imitated by using a dragged finish on a pale wood to create the linear effect characteristic of the birchwood grain.

Fake rosewood is good for "heavy" pictures, and fashionable too. It is created by washing a thin layer of black over a base of browny red. This finish suits many rooms furnished with dark antiques, but should be used in moderation so as not to overpower the room.

Bambooing of wood was a favourite art of the 18th century, when it was intimately linked with the fashion for all things Chinese. Imitation bamboo has long been recognized as one of the best fake finishes. Its charm lies in the characteristic grooves and ridges delicately painted onto the wood. Unlike the real thing, fake bamboo does not split. It is amusing and looks best on a rounded frame, using shades of amber, tan and straw to achieve a natural-looking effect, or following the lead of some of the more fantastical Regency interpretations, with colours such as grey-green and pink, or strongly contrasting blacks and reds.

With these sorts of painted fantasy, the effect is not supposed to look strictly like bamboo, rosewood or any other wood. The idea is to produce a finish that is pleasing and appropriate in its own right.

Tortoiseshell finishes can also be eyecatching, and can look very realistic. The base is usually bright – either orange or chrome yellow – with black shapes painted or fidgeted on, and then, while wet, feathered with a dry badger brush or feather. Once it is dry a sepia wash is painted over it and then sponged off while still damp, until the characteristic mottled look is achieved. Finally, varnish is applied. This technique can also be executed with distinctly un-tortoise-like colours.

Marbling is an appropriate embellishment for a frame if confined to a small scale. A light undercoat is applied, and then a further coat is loosely sponged over this. When the sponging is dry, streaks of colour are applied and then feathered to give the characteristic veining effect. Two or three different shades can be used in both the sponging and veining. The colours do not, of course, have to correspond with those of real marble: they can be as unrealistic as you like, as long as they suit the frame and picture.

the graining combs. Fine graining is sometimes used to imitate woods such as bird's eye maple, with its intricate whorls and smudges.

Birchwood was a popular wood in the 19th century, initially in France and then in Sweden, where it was

◀ There are no rules for creating fake effects: the finish can be as restrained or outrageous as you wish. 1. Rough tortoiseshell finish in cyclamen and black on a reverse frame. 2. Biedermeier frame in imitation birchwood with ochre dragging over a gesso base, and blacked corners. 3. Fantasy grained wood in emerald and grey. 4. Black rubbed over a red base to give the effect of dark rosewood. 5. Reverse frame with a tortoiseshell-like finish. 6. Rich finish resembling tortoiseshell, on an ochre base with an ochre slip and a terracotta border. 7. Ochre and blue fidgeted over a gesso base and flecked with tiny sections of gold leaf. 8. Marbled effect in blue-green with touches of grey, and cream veining. 9. Ivory-look finish on a gesso base with an inlaid section of gold over red bole. 10. Imitation porphyry created by applications of green and red over black, later stippled. 11. Lightly painted frame combining a marbled effect in cream and pale grey-green with stippled corner areas highlighted in fine green.

P lain lacquer frames are of two types: there are the factory-made mouldings which are suitable for posters and large prints, and there are hand-finished lacquer frames.

The factory-made frames are not usually real lacquer, but are wood frames that have been sprayed with colour and then treated with numerous coats of gloss varnish. They come in rich, deep colours such as red, green or blue, usually with a distinctive high-gloss finish. There is also a black finish, particularly suitable for Oriental pictures and often made up with an attractive fine gold edge.

The lacquering used on furniture involves a lengthy process requiring many coats of lacquer applied and polished over a long period of time. Although this process can be used on hand-finished lacquer frames it is not necessary – a frame does not have to take the sort of wear that a table or chest might and fewer coats of shellac, or a commercial varnish, are normally sufficient for a frame. They can be produced in a variety of colours and even in exotic semi-precious finishes imitating lapiz lazuli and malachite. Traditional colours such as rich black and deep Chinese red can look wonderful with Eastern works or other antique and slightly more exotic prints. Remember, though, that the hard gloss finish of lacquer can kill delicate works, so match the frame to a picture that is strong enough to be flattered by its bold surround.

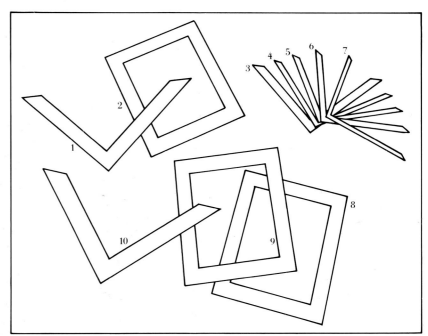

◄ These lacquer frames share a bright finish which is ideal for displaying bold pictures against the strong backgrounds of many modern settings. 1. Imitation lapiz lazuli on a shallow reverse frame in two shades of blue. 2. Shallow reverse frame of silver powder floated onto an undercoat of black. 3. Lacquered grey-brown manufactured finish with the colour applied as a wash so that the grain of the wood shows through. 4. Deep red manufactured lacquer finish on a narrow frame. 5. Narrow dark blue manufactured lacquer frame with a gold fillet. 6. Ivory-coloured manufactured lacquer finish on a narrow frame. 7. Dark green manufactured lacquer finish. 8. Lacquer frame hand-finished with gold and silver applied over a black base. The gold has been treated to give a goldfish-red effect and the silver is treated to appear green. 9. Gold-flecked black lacquer on a shallow reverse moulding. 10. Classic Chinese red lacquer over black with the red slightly distressed, and an inner edge of distressed gold leaf over black.

METAL FRAMES

The minimal clean lines of today's metal frames are ideal for modern, uncluttered homes and offices and for framing a whole range of bright posters, prints and reproductions.

Aluminium frames are now available in more shapes than ever. You are no longer restricted to the straight, flat, shiny gold-coloured frames that come in kit form. You can buy wider pieces, up to ¾-1in (2–2½cm) with a shiny or matt finish. Nor are they necessarily flat: those with a rounded profile give more depth and can be used on a wider variety of pictures.

These narrow aluminium mouldings, though lightweight, are strong and make ideal surrounds for large pictures, containing the image structurally as well as visually; whereas a thin wooden frame could not support the weight of a large picture.

The range of colours too, is wider now, with bronze, pewter, grey and black as alternatives to the traditional gold and silver.

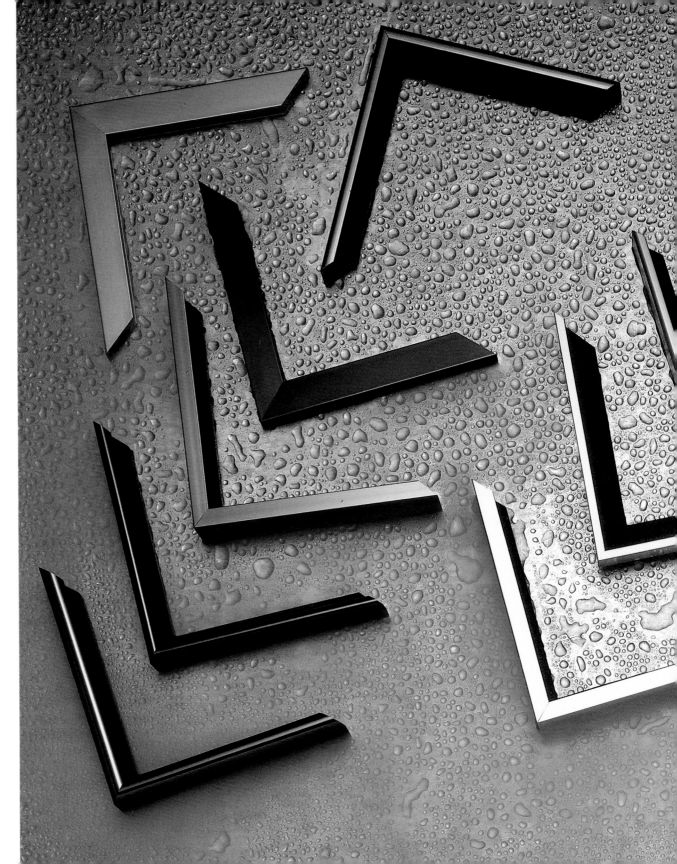

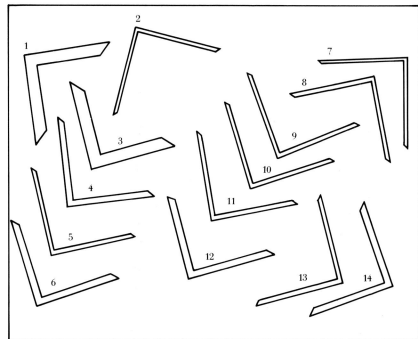

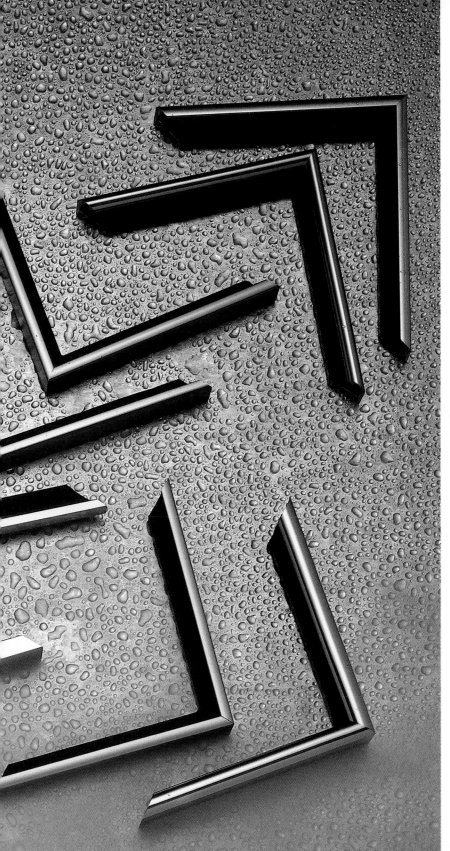

◀ Smart yet inexpensive, metal frames come in a wide range of attractive, unobtrusive modern finishes. 1. Flat frame with a highly-polished mirror-shined surface. 2. Small flat frame with a blue silver finish. 3. Flat-surfaced frame with a dark grey finish. 4. Deep moulding with a flat edge and a brown-bronze surface. 5. Narrow moulding finished in pink-bronze. 6. Rounded profile frame with a purple-grey finish. 7. Small flat frame with a classic silver finish. 8. Rounded profile frame with dark bronze finish. 9. Small frame with rounded profile and a high-shine gold surface. 10. Small, flat frame with a brown-bronze finish. 11. Very fine-profile frame with shiny gold finish. 12. Pale gold finish on a deep flat-surface frame. 13. Small, flat frame with frosted gold finish. 14. Deep frame with a rounded face and pale gold finish.

PICTURES
IN SITU

No matter how carefully a picture is framed, it
will lose its impact unless it is displayed in
sympathetic surroundings. The choice and
placing of a picture help to define the character
and mood of a room, as you will see in the
following pages. Each situation presents a
different challenge: a picture may complement
or contrast, surprise or reassure, but it should
always appear in harmony with its setting.

The placing of a picture is
of paramount importance.
Asymmetrical and proud,
this galactic pop singer
stands alone but is tied to
the uncompromising
furniture by a bust that
draws it back to earth.

It is one of the fundamental messages of this book that the framing and mounting of pictures can only be fully successful if they take due account of the picture's intended surroundings – the room where it is to be hung. In an art gallery pictures are the *raison d'être*: every aspect of the gallery is, or should be, designed to enhance our enjoyment of the art on display. In the home, however, there are competing claims on our attention. Even the most passionate collector would want to ensure that a painting, print or photograph does not totally dominate the living space; but neither should a picture of merit be devalued by being treated purely decoratively, as just a pattern, shape or colour accent. The ideal is to create an environment in which the pictures, fabrics, furniture and all the other objects in the room have a sense of inevitability and belonging, but in which the qualities of individual pictures can be properly appreciated when viewed in close up.

There are some basic considerations that apply regardless of the style and mood of the room or picture. Questions of proportion and balance are crucial. Is the work to be hung in a large or small area? The sort of frame appropriate for a high-ceilinged town house would look very much out of place in a small cottage. Scale is not just a private affair between the image, the mount and the frame: it must also take account of wall surfaces, furniture, nearby windows and many other factors.

The size and type of room will also affect the way you hang the picture. On the whole, if you have a small room with low ceilings, it is a mistake to hang several very large pictures closely ranked together.

Conversely, in a large room it is hard to make a group of small, rather insignificant pictures look good unless you reinforce their impact by exploiting other aspects of the interior – perhaps by hanging them purposely over a piece of furniture, or by showing them off in a corner alcove separated from the rest of the room.

Height is another critical issue. Wherever a picture is to be hung alone, the focus should generally be at eye level. But, of course, eye level is not a constant – it varies according to the layout and function of the

▲

In bold abstract works, colour values are all-important. In this closely grouped eye-level "frieze", the black pictures echo the sofa while the yellow forms a vibrant contrast. Although the daffodils are transient, other temporary yellow elements could be used to preserve the link with the yellow squares.

room. A group hung in a hallway will have a different level of focus from the same pictures hung opposite a sofa. Moreover, the eye-level rule takes no account of the way in which the eye can be directed by other objects placed near the picture – perhaps a sculpture placed against the wall or a wall-hung collection of ceramics.

Pairs and groups pose special difficulties of their own. Creating a well-balanced group requires patience and a good eye, taking colour values into account as well as scale. To give extra "weight" to one element of a composition, you might choose a darker or broader frame or one with a heavier appearance. Similar adjustments can be made by careful choice of mount. For example, two light-coloured watercolours hung vertically beside a large strong-toned print could seem lopsided: but you may be able to correct that impression by giving the pictures more emphatic frames or mounts than the larger print alongside.

The appeal of a group display can often be augmented by exploiting an interplay of shapes. It is surprising how dramatic an effect you can create by introducing a circle, oval or lozenge among squares and rectangles.

Wall treatments are of obvious importance in contributing to the impact a picture will make in the overall context of a room. It is not many years ago that plain white walls were *de rigueur* as an expression of modernist austerity. Recently, however, the pendulum has swung back in the direction of wallpapers, and otherwise decorated walls, which pose a different challenge to anyone attempting a picture display. Correctly used, wallpaper can enhance the pictures on show – for example, if you use a plain gold mount in the Victorian style to offset a rich floral wallpaper. The current fashion for stencilled friezes also offers excellent design options.

Choices about the overall mood or feel of a picture display will depend partly on personal taste and partly on the style of the room. Do not be afraid to opt for a heterogeneous group containing a mixture of media, periods, shapes and colours. It is all too easy to attach too much importance to rigid consistency: in the right setting, a casual, mixed display that evolves gradually over a period of time is just as valid as a formal arrangement in which the images, frames and mounts are all planned together to give a particular effect. If you do

choose a formal rather than an organic arrangement, remember that any future additions to the group may necessitate a total or partial re-think to accommodate them.

In placing pictures within a room there are, of course, practical aspects to consider as well as aesthetic concerns. If you can avoid it, you should not hang pictures opposite a window – or, at least, not in direct sunlight. Not only can direct sun harm the pigment but also, if the picture is glazed, the reflection of the window in the glass – or even in the varnish of an oil painting – can render the image obscure. The whole question of natural and artificial lighting is looked at in detail on pages 102–107.

This interior is a ▶ triumph of harmonious proportion. Black frames around the photographs underline their rectangular form, which contrasts with the emphatic roundness of the chairs. The palms seem to direct the eye to the pictures and are appropriate to their Egyptian subject matter. From this angle, even the ceiling fan plays its part in the overall balance of the arrangement.

▲
Above left Certain parts of the home are traditional sites for large works of art – for example, the wall above a sofa. The two pictures here make a definite contrast of scale, the smaller image deliberately lowered out of alignment to draw the eye to the table with its flowers and boxes. Here also is an example of using a broad, dark mount to increase the visual weight of a picture.

▲
A symmetrical arrangement is a good way of unifying pictures so that they neither conflict with, nor appear lost against, a strongly-patterned wallpaper. The pictures in this collection are stylistically and thematically linked, which unifies them further. Strong wood frames help to define the images and emphasize the distinction between paper and pictures.

▲
Dignified paintings in gold leaf frames are entirely appropriate in this formal room whose wallcoverings and the elaborate cartouche over the door convey a strong flavour of the past. The style of hanging also contributes to the period feel. The gold frames are sufficiently wide to contain the images so that they do not merge into the elaborate backdrop.

The Pomegranate wallpaper by William Morris and a William de Morgan vase create a strongly 19th-century atmosphere. The wistful expression of the woman in this simple black and white drawing — which belongs to the same period — is all the more poignant in such a rich and ornate setting. ▶

The colour of a room is usually determined by the colour of its walls or wall-covering. Assess whether the atmosphere is one of warmth and cosiness or bright modernity and choose pictures whose style and subject will suit the mood you have created.

The popularity of wallpaper has continued since the 18th century when it was first used on a wide scale. Styles have moved away from the heavy, ornate patterns of the past, although dark papers and a degree of patterning are enjoying a revival.

How to find coordinating or harmonizing colours is usually the main consideration when choosing pictures for a plain or faintly-patterned background, but more strongly patterned papers may present a greater challenge. Busy backgrounds need strong pictures and frames. A very gentle pastel or watercolour may be reduced to an insignificant interruption in a highly decorative or floral pattern.

If the paper has a regular pattern use this as a kind of frame for your pictures — for example, by hanging them within vertical or horizontal lines. The design of a papered background can be surprisingly successful in uniting a collection or disparate group of pictures.

Consider ways of tying pictures and wallcovering together — for example, choose a picture that complements the period feel of a room. Or you could echo the background by introducing one of its colours in the mount or frame. If you have a patterned fabric or textured background, you might be able to cover the mount in material of the same texture but in a plain colour which will not disappear into the background.

An ornate frame may not show to best advantage against a busy background but can be very effective against plain-coloured textured paper or fabric.

A painted wall is an ideal background for most pictures and frames. A dark wall provides a strong and dramatic setting but pictures hung on dark walls have to be inherently strong images, confidently framed. Any artificial lighting should be adjusted and strengthened to compensate for the lack of reflected light. Dark walls are especially good backdrops for monochrome works — pen and ink drawings or strong linear architectural prints.

Frames that have elaborate decorative finishes such as tortoiseshell, fake bambooing and other flagrantly false effects, can look very good grouped together on a dark wall. Gold, too, finds a natural home when backed by deep warm colours which enhance its richness and glow. A combination of differently-shaped frames, possibly with inner mounts wrapped in glowing silks or strongly textured and fibrous papers, shows to best advantage against a rich dark background colour which provides a strong setting without competing for attention.

A light-coloured wall is the best background for delicate watercolours, pastels and other fragile paintings that would be too easily absorbed into a wall with any depth of colour.

A pale wall need not necessarily have a pale frame. Choose one of medium strength, with a mid-weight mount if appropriate to the picture, but retain some of the subtlety of the pale background by repeating its colour in the mount, perhaps in a slip or as a thin wash line.

▼ Burgundy is a warm, mellow background colour, and works particularly well with gold frames. It is complemented here by red tones in the large central painting and by the red cushions among a group containing each of the main colours of that painting.

◀ Monochrome prints make an impact in this stark black and white setting, and maintain the architectural theme introduced by the tall white columns. The simple black frames are deliberately designed to merge with the background, projecting the pictures and preserving the two-tone effect.

Wood panelling provides a distinctive background for pictures but can make a small room look dark. Dark stained oak is still the most popular choice but local woods are sometimes used, either stained or left in their natural state and then waxed and polished. Limed panelling with its characteristic light grey tone is very common. Wood panels can be bleached to a warm yellow tint that with waxing takes on the appearance of honeyed wood.

Take stock of exactly how much light the panelling reflects: if it is particularly dark you may wish to highlight it with a gold-finished frame or bright gouache painting. Dark wood may introduce a period feel which you could perhaps emphasize with an evocative old oil.

The shape of the panels can act as a guide for arrangement. For example, if the panels are fairly long but narrow, you may choose to stress their length with a column of silhouettes. You needn't hang a square picture inside a square panel: a small round or oval can be just as effective and will introduce a pleasing contrast of shapes.

Both dark and light panelling take kindly to a quantity of pictures. Solitary works, unless they are large and commanding, can all too easily look lost against wood.

A mottled background ▶
can provide textural
interest without
clamouring for attention.
The dapple brown-red
tones of the walls and
similarly-toned fittings in
this bathroom make a
splendid foil for these
amusing cartoons and
decorative prints.

◀ A light wall throws these strong images into even stronger relief. Its cream painted base is enlivened by unusual red and beige speckling. The stencilled columns bring more colour to the wall and reinforce the architectural nature of the prints.

Plaster taken back to its ▶ near-natural state is wonderfully effective in reflecting the light onto the muted colours of this grey-toned picture. The pair of accompanying mirrors strongly echoes the architectural lines of the picture.

◄ Pale pictures and broad white and gold mounts compensate for the darkness of the wood panelling. The pictures are not arranged rigidly within the panels, but in three rows which extend as far down as the table. Bright ornaments and free-standing pictures on the table lend depth to the whole area, pushing the wall back to prevent an impression of flatness.

◄ Two pairs of pictures evenly spaced within these long upper panels create an impression of height. Their pale green mounts lighten the dark stained panelling and match the green rafters above. Striking use has been made of the large panel that houses an oil, not framed, but painted fresco-like onto the wood itself, the edges of the panel acting as a natural picture frame.

M ost rooms receive some sunlight for at least a part of the day. It would seem to be a natural bonus for lighting pictures, but it may turn out to be an enemy rather than a friend. The greatest disadvantage of natural daylight — even the so-called weak Northern daylight — is that it can badly harm pigment and fade watercolours and other pictures painted in fragile media. It can also lighten a wall itself, leaving faded patches around the area where a picture might once have hung.

A glazed painting will usually reflect glare if it is hung opposite a window, and much, if not all of the detail will be lost. Some glossy oil paints and varnishes can be similarly affected. Bright light can also cause objects in the room to be reflected in the glass. Non-reflective glass can reduce glare on prints, watercolours and so on, but is unattractive, and obviously no use on oils and tempera which are normally left unglazed. Ideally, keep delicate pictures out of direct light and rely instead on the light that in pale-toned rooms will bounce around from one light wall to another.

A sheer curtain will diffuse the light passing through a window and allow the detail in a picture to be seen while protecting its colours from bright light.

Daylight can enhance some pictures: you could use dramatic shadows to emphasize a striking modern work, and if you have a skylight you may even be able to contrive an effect whereby the light falls across the picture in an unusual and eye-catching way. Observe the effect of light on the wall at different times of the day, in order to see how it may affect a particular picture.

Artificial lighting can be used

either to bring out with curatorial seriousness the quality of a work or to provide a dramatic effect at night, entirely changing the look of a room and its pictures. Take into account the mood of the lit room when deciding which pictures to hang in it — for example, an extrovert open-air scene may not be in keeping with a cosy, mellow atmosphere.

The most common type of artificial lighting for the home is the ordinary household tungsten bulb:

shielded by some kind of shade, which is usually translucent, it casts a warm and pleasant general light but is not suitable for highlighting individual pictures. Remember, though, not all pictures warrant the emphasis that special lighting provides, while others simply do not lend themselves to being strongly lit.

If you have a group of pictures or a collection, you needn't necessarily light them all: you may decide to light only the central work or the

largest. Alternatively, you may wish to highlight one or two of the smaller works that might otherwise be overlooked.

The classic method of lighting specific pictures is with the traditional picture light. This can be attached to the top or bottom of a picture, or on the wall just above the frame. It is probably best placed above the picture where it can give supplementary lighting to any objects and furniture beneath it, whereas lighting a picture from below will only cast extra, unnecessary light on the ceiling.

Picture lights usually come in a brass or metallic finish. They can be angled to overcome any glare, but if the glass or varnish is still giving off a reflection, tilt the picture slightly toward the floor to reduce at least some of the glare.

Make sure that the fitting is wide enough to illuminate the whole picture: as a guide, the light should usually be two thirds of the picture's width. If you have a particularly long picture, place the fitting slightly further than usual from the top or bottom of the frame, so that the beam will extend along the entire length of the work.

Low-voltage tungsten-halogen spotlights can be employed for specific directional spotlighting. These are small and discreet and can either be fitted directly into the ceiling or mounted on a track fitted onto the ceiling. If you are having lights fitted, remember that, although you may only have one picture now, you may well acquire more later, so it is worthwhile leaving your options open by having several spots fitted at once, or a longer track installed than you might need at the time. These lights are best used in conjunction with other light directed upward from

Abstract works offer more scope for manipulating daylight imaginatively, as shown by the two examples here.

◀ *Far left* The glass reflects the bright daylight from the slatted venetian blinds, lending depth to a picture with fairly muted colours, hanging alone on a plain white wall.

◀ The reflected shadows of the slatted window frame cast geometric bars across this picture, reinforcing its linear nature. The effect is doubly dramatic against the sky background of the picture.

the ground or table level so that the rest of the room does not appear dark by comparison with the spotlit pictures.

There are also portable, adjustable uplighters. These can be hidden on the floor, or behind a piece of furniture, so that the source of light is disguised.

As a general rule, strong directional light should strike your pictures at an angle of 60° from the horizontal in order to prevent shadows being cast by the frame and to minimize the reflections of a glazed picture. If there is seating near the pictures, check that the light does not subject the sitter to glare.

Washing a wall with light is a relatively new technique that is ideal for a large work or a whole wall of pictures. A wall can be washed with either a concealed fluorescent strip or with the more flexible recessed downlighters or concealed portable uplighters. These all produce a soft, even wash

of light but are only effective on walls with matt finishes.

Fluorescent light gives a more accurate rendition of a picture than tungsten-halogen bulbs. However, watercolours and pastels deteriorate in ultraviolet light, so have a filter fitted to prevent damage to paintings and delicate works.

▲
A change of atmosphere is brought about by firelight and the romantic glow of candles. The light has been contrived so that the flowers cast shadows on the wall in echo of the inbuilt shadows in the picture.

A wall is lit only where ▶ there is a painting so that the image stands out from the recess in sharp relief to the subdued lighting in other parts of the room.

Far right A traditional ▶ picture light is in keeping with this period painting. Its matt brass finish has been chosen to match the frame.

◀ Spotlights need not light a whole picture. Adjustable recessed minispots in the ceiling dramatically highlight just two parts of this Oriental screen, defining areas of fine detail and lending depth and richness to the whole design.

◀ *Far left* An adjustable ceiling spot with a white surround to blend with the ceiling, has been carefully angled to highlight the central part of the picture. Alternative or supplementary lighting is provided by the two angled lights above the bed. Mirrors double the amount of light given out by the recessed spots in the display units.

Pictures must often take their place as part of an overall scheme in which other considerations, such as comfort, play a major part in the arrangement of the room. And it is an important precept of interior design that pictures work with the furniture, not against it, to create an effect of harmony.

One way to achieve such sympathy between pictures and furniture is to relate them through tone, style, material or period. Even if there is no obvious link, you could align the pictures with the furniture in a symmetrical arrangement that suggests balance and unity. The elements of the group need not be symmetrical in themselves – ovals, rectangles and squares will all work together, as long as the overall effect is balanced.

If you are framing a picture in wood, the colours and shades of furniture and artpieces need not necessarily echo one another, but they could share some tones. Try to choose a wood that blends with the furniture, or a mount that matches a colour in your curtains or armchair. Pieces from the same period, of course, work well together. A large modern oil looks good above a sofa in today's plain simple lines, and groups of 19th-century watercolours will flatter a Victorian mantelpiece. Contrasts of period can be exciting and dramatic, but harder to achieve without some practice.

A balance between the relative weights of pictures and furniture is important when arranging a group. A dramatic heavy oil would over-

▲ These reticent prints, simply and identically mounted and framed, introduce a feeling of space and simplicity in this busy room, with pattern and colour on every surface. A lamp and screen fill the empty areas on either side of the lower pictures and provide a link between the austere monochrome statement and the vivid mélange beneath.

A botanical motif provides ▶ an appropriate and decorative thematic link between pictures and furniture in this country cottage. The central fabric collage, with its fabric mount, extends far down the wall, nearly touching the flowered needlework cushions below.

power a light wicker table, whereas the massed colours and graphic lines of a strong theatre poster would echo the weight of a chest or sofa.

Pictures can also work with furniture to create a lively area from a nondescript space. A corner seating arrangement with a chair or two and a low table can be distinctly defined with a strong picture on each corner wall, hung low enough to draw the eye to the area.

Pictures can give a new importance to an ordinary piece of furniture. A large picture or group hung above a double bed that lacks a headboard can totally alter its appearance.

Once you have chosen a display that suits the furniture, consider the balance between the pictures themselves, as well as that between pictures and furniture: they should be close enough to stand together as a group, without seeming crowded.

An important but often overlooked point is that the perimeter of the group as a whole should not extend beyond the perimeters of the furniture beneath, or the eye will no longer make the connection.

A direct way to unite furniture and pictures as part of a whole decorative design – especially if your collection does stray beyond these boundaries – is through objects and ornaments. For example, tablelamps, candlesticks and vases all provide vertical links between pictures and furniture, leading the eye from one group to the other, and can also introduce variations of shape and scale which improve the whole arrangement.

◄ Only distinctive images could sit confidently above this imposing pier table. These two stern artistic prints lend weight to the ornate chairs beneath them and prevent the table from being dominating. The radiating diagonals of the images give the composition movement.

The wood of the polished ▶
floorboards is echoed in the
furniture and frames to
make a unified group whose
strength offsets the highly
decorative background.
The lamp and vase give
height and substance to
the table and connect the
pictures to each other and
the furniture.

A symmetrical grouping ▶
which exploits an emphatic
contrast of scale. The
miniatures on the wall
form a link with the small
brushes and bottles on the
table; while the portrait
shape of the lowest picture,
neatly ties the two groups
together. The whole
arrangement is anchored
from below by the dark
wood of the chest, and
bordered above by an
attractive painted bow.

◀ Old black and white prints share the period feel of the graceful furniture. The group extends beyond the contours of the table, but unity of design has been preserved in an arrangement which cleverly echoes the outline of the mirror. A further link is provided by the central picture, strongly mounted and framed in wood to match the furniture.

▲
Boldness and humour are the keynotes of this group. The distinctive decorative prints are connected to the sideboard by a splendid Victorian dome of birds. Balance has been maintained by raising the central row to encompass the dome and by framing and mounting the prints identically.

Any type of object, whether purely ornamental or primarily functional, can be successfully combined with pictures provided you take into account their relative weights and styles. Some ornaments make delightful complements to a grand picture or collection but others deserve more than to serve as foils: if you have an important sculpture or work of art that demands attention, place it near the picture but in a space of its own. Consider using unusual ornaments in places where you may not normally expect to see them: found objects such as sea-sculpted driftwood can be positioned on the wall in a group or interspersed among sympathetic works of art. Other decorative objects can be scattered on tables nearby or grouped together beneath some pictures to make a compact and unified composition.

A suitable starting point for combining pictures with objects might be to find a basic decorative principle that unites them, perhaps a shared theme, colour or pattern. For example, muskets and medals would sit well beneath military paintings, and sporting trophies would be the ideal complement for sporting prints. If colour is the linking principle try to use a range of shades and tones rather than restricting yourself to a laboured collection of rigidly matched items.

Similarity of texture or material is another way of achieving a sympathetic relationship — for example, by placing copper pots beneath a beaten copper frame or a needlework cushion beneath a piece of framed fabric.

Living objects depicted in paintings, such as flowers and fruit, can be very effective when emphasized by the real thing nearby.

Objects can be framed and hung on the wall like paintings, or their irregular three-dimensional outlines could be used to break up the geometry of a group of pictures. When arranging objects on a shelf or table a cohesive display can be achieved by occasionally allowing the object to reach up as far as a picture frame, and by slightly overlapping some of the shapes so that a fluid line of movement is maintained. A composition can seem disjointed if there is too much space between the elements.

Unframed objects need not necessarily be consigned to a safe position on a nearby table: you could have shelves made to align with existing pictures or to act as an extension of a mantelshelf. Pedestals can be used to display small sculptures and pots and provide decorative interest at interim levels.

◀ Attention is drawn to this small view of houses by a heavy brown frame and large objects. The white of the lamp and candlestick on either side acts as a kind of secondary frame. The picture has eyelets, but such a delicate work may be lost hung on a large wall and instead benefits from the proximity of substantial ornaments.

This corner seating area is an elaborate system of balances in which pictures and objects are given equal emphasis. The whinnying horses and serene Oriental portraits make two complementary sets of twins. The horses' irregular outline links them to the bizarre mask, which makes a joint polychrome statement with the

adjacent modern abstract. ▶ Subdued tones are woven through the composition — black in the speakers, table, cushions and pot; brown in the horses, praying monk and upholstery; the two strands meeting in the largest picture and its frame. Downlighters concealed behind the pelmet create a dramatic effect at night.

◀ These pictures are brought to life by two tiers of shells ranged beneath them. Plain mounts and minimal frames project the images and give them a solidity to match that of their real counterparts.

Copious flowers provide an ▶ appropriate natural flourish linking the paintings with the real and ceramic fruit below. Uplighters bring a modern note to this traditional set and cast a warm glow over the whole ensemble.

This chronological chart ▶ of the kings and queens of England is well served by the imperious couple who guard the wooden chest and share its deep red tones. Tall oars maintain the wood theme and redress any imbalance between the imposing chest and the less substantial display.

Far right, top The ▶ naiveté of form and colour in the painting that presides over this group is echoed in the primitive painted style of the cupboard and the crudely colourful bust.

Far right, bottom The ▶ temptation to clutter has been resisted in favour of an understated arrangement. Pieces of bark, with jagged edges, seem to dance around this fabric giving a touch of vivacity to an otherwise static and linear performance.

◀ This picture is hung off centre to draw attention to the staircase and is balanced by a chair whose sheen matches the tones of both print and skirting. Decoration is kept to a minimum so that this simple, unusual pair becomes the focal point in a large modern hall.

H alls and staircases are almost domestic art galleries. Historically, halls and landings in grand homes were used to display massive works and even in today's lesser spaces they provide an excellent opportunity for making an eye-catching display.

The hall is the first room that people see on entering a home and it sets the tone and atmosphere of the surroundings. As it is designed to be walked along, the pictures are guaranteed attention, so make them tempting and dramatic – a taste of things to come.

Pictures in a hall are not seen constantly, as they are in a living room, so you can have them in some quantity without fear that they will overwhelm. You can also be bolder and stronger in your choice.

People do not often sit in halls so the pictures should be hung at eye level, although if the layout is appropriate, you could provide one or two chairs for prospective viewers.

To climb a staircase can be a positive pleasure if the walls are lined with interesting pictures. The sense of ascent and descent gives an opportunity to arrange pictures in a vibrant way. Hang them in parallel rising lines so that on each rise of the stair, the eye falls naturally on another picture. Make sure that the most striking ones are not wasted: hang them at the top and bottom of the staircase where they will be seen from the hall even when the stairs are not being used.

Large pictures can look impressive on a staircase wall, particularly if it is a grand one, but on a smaller, conventional staircase where space is limited, avoid having too many large works. If you *are* using big pictures, however, make sure there are smaller ones interspersed among them.

Spiral and grand curving staircases offer excellent opportunities for surprise as you round the corner.

Open-tread staircases and those where both floors can be seen at the same time should have strong pictures on the upper level to beckon to anyone standing below.

Halls and staircases are perfect for pictures that have a consistent theme – for example, a historical collection or series of book plates, as the eye is carried naturally along the wall when the viewer passes from one room or level to another. Small tables in the hall or on a landing can also be used to display any artefacts that are part of the collection.

You can introduce drama with specific directional lighting such as spots or tracks for pictures in the hall and downlighters or picture lights on the stairs, combined with overall lighting to enable people to see where they are going. Consider using wall lights, which will interfere less with a display than the conventional pendant at top and bottom.

◀ The arrangement of these pictures together with their hard, square frames accentuates the shape of the curved wall. The gilded eagle at the foot of the stairs guards the ornithological collection grouped along the staircase. Modern directional spots and a hanging glass pendant spread a bright but warm welcoming glow.

▲
A 19th-century town house is an apt home for a group of studied plasterwork details, set on rich blue fabric which matches the carpet below and the blue detailing of the plaster. Rectangles, ovals and squares form balanced displays within classic gold frames hung on bands of ribbon of the same blue as the mounts. Each row is hung in precisely graded lines along the staircase.

▲
More plasterwork medallions are hung in the hall on the wall opposite the staircase — a preface to the story that continues up the stairs. They are similarly mounted and framed but in bigger groups to suit the larger space provided by the wall. The groups are arranged symmetrically on either side of an ornamental mirror that increases the sense of space and light.

◀ A passage which leads into a garden is a good place for hanging a collection of antique rural implements. An unexpected picture hung above the dado in an appropriate wood frame raises the eye beyond the rake and scythe to give an impression of height to the narrow hallway.

◄ In keeping with the staircase — an architectural feature in its own right — the pictures in the hall seem to travel upward toward another display on the landing. On the lower level they complement the emphatically linear look of the modular panels of the stairwell walls, the slatted upper bannister and the horizontal lines made by the stairs themselves. Minimal, unobtrusive frames and white mounts maintain the modern style of the setting and unify the large number of pictures in the hall which spill over into the living room. The hall is well supplied with natural light but downlighters are used to draw the eye toward the upper level.

◀ A detail from the same staircase showing a collection of black and white prints, whose monochrome tones complement the two-tone stairs. They have been arranged with the darkest innermost, becoming progressively lighter as they emerge from behind the stairs.

▲
An exercise in stately proportion, this small, ornate chimneypiece has been ennobled by an elegant, comely display of symmetrically arranged portraits and ornaments. The theme of grandeur is maintained from above by elaborate plaster work, and from below by the coats of arms that fill the panels on either side of the fireplace. The central picture has been raised slightly to accommodate the arrangement on the mantelshelf that connects all the elements in the design, both vertically toward the central picture, and horizontally by using two blue lamps on stands as if they were a continuation of the mantel shelf.

▲
The virtue of this striking arrangement is its simplicity. The round silhouettes in their square black frames precisely echo the circular medallions within the fireplace, also set in black. The mirror reflects portraits on the opposite wall which match the one hung alongside the mantelpiece.

The simple scene depicted ▶ in this painting preserves the rustic feel of the room. The painting hangs very low in the absence of a mantelshelf, but is not as casually placed as it seems: the eye is led from the picture to the candle holder mounted near the bottom of the picture to a stately bust on a pedestal, all three linked by the stone surround.

The wall above a fireplace is a traditional location for displaying pictures. The fireplace is such a definite piece of "furniture" that it always attracts notice and anything displayed above it is assured of immediate attention.

Often just one large picture is displayed centrally above a fireplace but in a grand or formal room it is not uncommon to see one large central picture flanked by tiers of smaller ones.

There is plenty of scope for arranging pictures with both vertical and horizontal formats, provided you take into account the whole chimney breast including the fireplace itself. The pictures hung above a mantelpiece do not have to fill the space completely but they do have to balance the bulk below the mantelpiece.

You should also consider the material of which the fireplace is made, as you may be able to use it as a basis for decorative links with the pictures: marbled paper in a mount could make an interesting echo of a marble fire surround, whereas black cast iron might suggest a silhouette or simple black frame. Any pictures used in this area should be strong enough to stand up to the imposing architecture of the fireplace.

If you decide to use a mirror instead of, or in addition to, pictures, check what you will see reflected in it from the opposite wall. Whether it is another picture or just wallpaper, you will want the reflection to look right with the fireplace and any pictures above it.

If you have a mantelshelf use objects placed along it to draw the eye from the fireplace up to the pictures: vases, candlesticks, a sculpture or even another picture

▲

The theme of this old French poster, given a solo position above a Victorian fireplace, is echoed by the ornamental fruit and fruit motifs on the bowl and jug among the objects that liaise between picture and fireplace. The poster shares tones with the ragged wall, the pine fireplace surround and the screen to make a varied but unified composition.

propped against the wall, will all serve to connect shelf and pictures together. Remember when you hang your pictures to allow for the height of any objects that are to sit on the shelf beneath.

If the fireplace is in use, check whether your picture is in any danger from gas fumes or the dirt from an open fire. Hang pictures high enough to avoid such problems, or make sure they are properly protected if there is the slightest risk of damage.

▲

This solitary botanical print, highlighted by an intricate washed mount and an unusual gilded frame with mirrored sections, introduces a bright spray of colour in an otherwise subdued scheme. On the mantelshelf the varied collection including ceramic animals, family photographs and an icon spills over like gentle tears on either side.

◀ A prominent feature has been made of an unassuming marble-surround fireplace. Ornaments and pictures rise in pairs from the floor upward and outward toward the fan-shaped paintings in each recess. The large central mirror has an elaborately painted surround which acts as a frame for the pictures reflected in it. In the small space beneath, a carriage clock has been deliberately used instead of a traditional mantelclock which would overwhelm the ensemble. In the space above the mirror, which hangs low over the mantelshelf in order to maintain the balance between the elements, is a delicate classical grouping of musical instruments, painted directly onto the wall, and leading the eye further up still toward the cornice.

◀ The alcove into which this fireplace is set provides a natural frame for a self-contained display, dominated by the elaborate wood surround of the mantelpiece. The piscatorial carvings along the mantelshelf are echoed in the nautical display that contains a sea monster and a fish among the ornaments on the shelf, and ship paintings on the wall above and on either side. The composition is compact, the pictures hanging so low down that the creatures hardly seem removed from their natural habitat. A wooden beam and wooden furniture contain the display, reinforcing its unified impact.

◀ An interesting juxtaposition of contrasting styles and media lends style to this simple rough-finished chimney breast. The central oil, whose colours complement the wood mantelpiece, is flanked by two Chinese paintings on fabric. The combination owes its success to the grouping of the pictures within a rectangle as a collection of very different portraits. Their relationship is further emphasized by the variety of objects on the shelf, with their contrastingly irregular outline. Although the central portrait hangs on a disguised fixture an elaborate tasselled cord seems to hold it in place, giving it due prominence and lending height to the group.

When considering where to hang pictures, do not rule out the less traditional locations in the house. The more mundane parts of the home, even the bathroom or lavatory, can provide a suitable space for ornamentation.

You can choose pictures that tie in with the function of a room – for example, images of fruit or vegetables will suit a kitchen – and the unexpectedness of the location will ensure that the picture gets more, rather than less, attention. Rooms not lived in, such as cloakrooms, are often characterless and anonymous places: collections of photographs, old prints and cartoons are ideal here to create a warm, personal atmosphere.

In a small room or one where functional items take up valuable wall space, you may have to be more imaginative in your choice of position. Make use of any architectural features, such as doors, archways and woodwork. Utilize any available surface, including the floor and even the ceiling. Pictures can be hung on cupboards and wardrobes, or they can be propped on shelves, rested against books and even placed under the glass top of a dressing table. If the room is very small, use mirrors to double the impact. Position pictures to create a sense of surprise: a painting hung over a door will not be seen by someone first entering the room but will be noticed as they turn around. If you have a room under a sloping roof, choose a picture that is bright

These piscatorial prints ▶ are hung unusually low – perfectly placed for bathtub level viewing. Stencilled motifs and ornamental fish maintain the underwater theme.

enough to stand out from the shadow cast by the slanted ceiling.

If you are hanging pictures in a functional room, consider how its working role might affect certain media – for example, a delicate pastel might suffer from the steamy atmosphere of a bathroom. Prints, posters and reproductions are often the best choices for these situations.

You should not relegate the least interesting of your pictures to such rooms – after all, they are just as much the fabric of the house as the rooms that visitors will see first.

◄ A set of pictures hung above a door, as these prints are, fills the usually dead space between door and ceiling and makes a room appear taller than it really is. The centre pictures are framed in antique, distressed gold leaf; while the outer frames are of distressed gilt with mirrors set in the panels to give a generally light impression.

◄ This society beauty fits surprisingly well in this kitchen, partly because they share a period feel. The picture is a valued work and is thus placed out of reach of harmful steam and smoke.

▲ Lavatories are popular locations for full and cheerful displays that are guaranteed attention. This bright family group has been arranged to enliven the unusual entrance.

A picture on its own can be more difficult to display than a group, especially if it is of only moderate size and conventional in style. You will have to decide whether it is to be the focal point of the room or an element that blends in with the interior design scheme. It is, as ever, a question of giving a picture enough decorative importance without overstating it.

A picture may stand out by virtue of its size or unconventional subject matter, but you can help to emphasize it with confident framing and careful positioning. Many pictures deserve this solo treatment, but they must be strong enough to stand up to close scrutiny.

A single picture needn't look lost: it can be tied in with the rest of the room. One way to do this is to link it thematically with the furniture. To highlight a picture's importance you can create a special area for it in which architectural features and furniture are used to provide extra emphasis. For example, hanging a picture just above a sofa ties seating and walls together and makes a feature of the whole area. This is particularly effective where the tones and colours of the picture reflect those of the furniture below. Similarly, an unnoticed corner or alcove can be brought into the body of the room by the hanging of an appropriate and attention-catching picture.

An effective way to dramatize a single picture is to exploit contrasts of style. For example, a gold-framed evocative old oil can look surprisingly vibrant in a modern room minimally decorated.

A picture doesn't have to be on a wall to draw attention to itself: unconventional approaches are becoming increasingly popular, with the frame standing on a mantelpiece or against a wall, or even supported by a stool or easel.

◀ This strong graphic image, which catches the attention with an unexpected splash of colour in a modern, monochrome setting, is all the more striking for not having a counterpart. An apt and witty choice, it depicts the famous chair by Rietveldt, itself a modern classic of its time.

▲
A busy, colourful composition enlivens a severe setting. The lamp acts as a kind of three-dimensional extension of the picture, bringing it firmly into the room.

◀ Only a big, strong picture could fill a large recess such as this without appearing lost. The bright modern painting fits neatly into the alcove which acts as a substitute frame. The ornaments beneath anchor the picture and the strategically placed lamp picks out its bold, black lines, linking it to the stained wood table.

◀ A famous photograph by Man Ray has been well placed on an easel-height table whose legs echo the shape of the swirls on the nude's back. The unconventional method of display accords well with the unusual column and bust and ensures that the picture will not be overlooked in this busy room.

▲ A large, single picture can transform a plain, empty area and in this case provides an amusing visual joke: a solid, three-dimensional chair brings to life those represented in the image, blurring the distinction between art and reality. An optical illusion has been created by hanging the picture just above the ground to suggest an additional level.

▲ A single elegant period painting such as this can lend surprising grandeur to an uncluttered modern setting. The impression that the picture is centrally placed has been created by using the alcove as a kind of mount, leaving more space below the portrait than above it. A gentle spotlight set into the ceiling emphasizes both picture and frame.

▲ A picture that does not lend itself to being paired with another could be teamed instead with an object that will not detract from its solo status. The proud oval portrait of Lord Herbert of Cherbury staring out from a recess above a panelled dado is linked by the frame's ornate gilding to the unusual and equally stately bust below, dressed in gilded lace.

A large picture is often most effective when hung in solitary splendour. The sheer size of this bird and the flamboyance of its plumage would cast an ornithological pall over less extrovert creatures. The chair covering and flowers echo the foliage and plumage, but the bird preserves its independence by standing proudly over one side of the table rather than conventionally over the centre. ▶

▲
A whole wall has been allocated to each of these paintings, so that they are given the prominence of single pictures instead of a pair. An old pestle and mortar and a pot of grape-carrying cherubs lead the eye to the fruitbowl on the wall. Two traditional rural symbols flank the pastoral painting above the seat.

Matching mounts and identical heavy dark frames flatter the light tones of these flower paintings reinforcing the similarities between them and giving them sufficient weight to stand above the cast iron fireplace. The contrast between the pictures and their frames is repeated in the juxtaposition of the bright 19th-century decorative tiles adorning the sides of the mantelpiece.

This stepped pair has been created by using matching mounts and frames to emphasize similarities of tone, size and period between the pictures. The wood frames match the furniture and the connection is reinforced by the decorative treatment on one of the frames causing the eye to leap toward it from the marquetry-decorated ornaments on the table. The pair is linked from above by a lamp with a metal base to echo the distressed gold of the frames.

Far right Here the eye is drawn immediately to the mounts and frames surrounding these very different Japanese pictures. Intricate designs of Oriental influence cover each mount, the patterns cleverly varied to complement the variation in the pictures. Identical frames lead the eye from one picture to the other in confirmation of the relationship between them.

S ome pictures fall into natural pairs by virtue of a shared subject or style: botanical prints or fashion plates are obvious candidates for being paired, especially as colours are often repeated within a set. If you have a print which is not part of of a pair, it will often be surprisingly easy to find a similar one to team it up with.

If you have two pictures which share some similarities but are of different scale, you could pair them by using a similar treatment on their mounts and frames. The sizes of the mounts can vary but you should use frames of the same dimensions to create the optical illusion that the pictures are actually the same size.

When choosing the colour of the mount for two dissimilar pictures with the same subject matter — perhaps two outdoor scenes or two wild flower prints — you could either pick out a colour that appears in both pictures or one that appears in neither but complements both. The frames in this case, of course, must match.

Pictures that have little in common but their size can be paired by using mounts of a colour that appears in both pictures, or that blends in well with each of them, tying them together. Dissimilar pictures can sometimes be paired by their position in relation to each other: they needn't be the same size, or even share a common theme but

could simply be hung as a pair, with tops, bottoms or edges aligned.

If you have a pair of pictures that are so alike as to be almost identical, you might wish to introduce some element of variety, perhaps in the mount or by using decorative marquetry in only one of a pair of wooden frames. Take care that you do not make them dramatically different from each other: slight variations create interest but you should keep disproportion under control.

A pair of pictures need not stand like two sentry-boxes together. They can be hung quite far apart as long as there is some link between them and can even be used successfully on either side of quite a large group of pictures, bordering and tying the group together.

If the pair or pairs are symmetrically arranged, try to put them with some asymmetrical feature in the vicinity so that the overall impression is not too rigid. A stepped arrangement can work well, creating a diagonal which gives liveliness and movement, possibly echoing a staircase on an opposite wall. You could even position an ornament or a lamp in the space beneath the upper picture to suggest that the picture was forced upward to accommodate it.

Pairs of pictures often work well together with furniture that comes in pairs: a complete group can be made of a pair of chairs topped by two pictures similarly mounted and framed. A grand pair of candelabra or candlesticks can be ennobled by matching pictures above them.

▲
The severe lines of the classically modern furniture in this room could create a harsh and unwelcoming atmosphere, but the pair of large framed plans on the wall have a softening effect on the overall scheme. The plans are hung very close together in identical mounts and frames, as if they were two halves of the same picture — the top half complementing the large circular Fortuny light and the lower half sharing the definite lines of the chairs which intersect its design. In their content and arrangement both halves pay tribute to the importance of architectural principles in this room.

Two very different modern ▶ pictures, with their top edges aligned to suggest a pair, complement the high tech image of this work unit. The pictures work together more for their connection with the furniture than for any similarity between them: monochrome tones predominate on the desk and in the large picture; while the narrow blue frame of the smaller print ties in with the deep blue chair.

◀ These rich flower prints have enough in common to allow for subtle variations in the mounts to suit each picture without destroying their partnership. The different formats of the framed pictures reflect the shape of each composition. One print centred above another, the pair is ideally placed to complement the pillows, and the rich chintz curtains whose colours and theme they share.

The members of any group of pictures should seem to belong naturally together and should therefore be hung fairly close to each other so that the eye can make the connection. Where the pictures are restrained in style or colour you need leave only a minimal space between them, but bright and busy pictures need more space around them.

Picture arranging is often a case of trial and error. Try out different arrangements on the floor until you achieve the right balance between colour, proportion and interest.

As a starting point you could arrange the pictures within the conventional groupings discussed below but bear in mind that these are guidelines rather than rules, and pleasing effects are often achieved by unorthodox arrangements which work well despite, or even thanks to their deliberate flouting of tradition.

A popular approach is to arrange the pictures so that their centres align along an imaginary horizontal line fixed at eye level. Or you could arrange them so that pictures sit above and below such a line. The line relates the pictures but permits a certain informality. The same is true of pictures grouped around a central vertical line. You could have several columns arranged in this way; these need not be the same shape as each other, but each line

This interesting ►
arrangement takes its cue
from a horizontal base line.
The pictures are arranged
in a pyramid shape with
one heavy oil at the apex to
counterbalance a full row
below. The group is
anchored from above by a
display shelf at cornice
level housing a group of
patterned plates.

should have a similar overall weight.

If you have a range of different styles and sizes, the simplest way to give them some form is to align the tops of the upper row of pictures and allow the others to range freely below. Use the largest works for the top row to anchor the smaller ones. A less common application of this principle is to group pictures so that the base line is fixed and the group rises casually above it.

The outer edges of a group can be arranged to form a rectangle or square with other pictures placed within those perimeters. This works with pictures of equal shape and size, and with mixed groups in which the interplay between shapes and spaces takes place freely within the perimeters formed by the frames of the outer pictures. Following similar principles, you could also arrange groups of equal or unequal size within a band, to form a kind of frieze (see page 92).

Another device is to balance the pictures around an imaginary cross drawn through the centre of the group to give a freer form than many rigidly symmetrical arrangements.

If you have one particularly large picture among a mixed group hang it centrally as a pivot for smaller works ranged around it. This gives you the flexibility to add new pictures or rearrange them easily.

◀ This grouping overcomes, and makes a virtue of, the limitations imposed by a narrow area. A sense of space is created by using the full width of the wall but not its whole length, in a symmetrical arrangement based on the classic cross shape, with the larger pictures at top and bottom.

▲
Mixed media are happily
combined in this simple but
pleasing group based on a
symmetrical columnar
arrangement. The pictures
are hung close together but
generous mounts ensure
that each retains its
individuality.

▲
A group that takes into
account the table and the
pictures at floor level. The
central column is anchored
from above by the dignified
black and white print,
echoed by two more large
works which weight the
outer columns from below.

This widespread, diverse ▶
group is clearly successful,
despite its blatant defiance
of convention. Shades of
blue provide colour interest
and unite the group, hung
to accommodate the
furniture whose forms
offset the right-angled
display above.

▲
A modern group toplined
below the outer frame of
the picture rail. Smaller
pictures are hung low down
the wall for closer
appreciation, and are
contained within the
borders made by the upper
row of larger, more
outspoken works.

Here, the symmetry ▶
created by the centre
column and bottom row is
strong enough not to be
disturbed by the disparity
of format between the
upper corner pictures.
Each cushion on the sofa is
placed to continue the
tones of the row behind.

Collections of pictures, memorabilia and other artefacts are very personal, fascinating and often revealing statements of their owners' likes and dislikes. With time, they may even become a kind of portable museum, perhaps recording significant family events, or commemorating a lifetime's devotion to a sport or keen interest.

For a collection to work, whether it comprises pictures, artefacts or a combination of two- and three-dimensional elements, the individual items will have something that links them to each other in some way. Perhaps they are all works by the same artist, or they may share a common theme, from ships to houses or battles. They may celebrate a period or event, or use

The weight of these ▶ two rigid rows of dominant, identically-framed architectural prints is echoed and counterbalanced by the striped fabric of the sofa which fills the space beneath the collection.

▲
This clutch of collections ranging across every surface is united by a Japanese screen. Order is preserved by arranging the pictures within fairly strict lines.

These Pre-Raphaelite ▶ pictures, unmounted and identically framed, constitute an uncluttered gallery-like collection, with plenty of space to stand back and admire.

the same medium – for example, charcoal, pastels or ink. Whatever the theme, it is important that they be displayed close together to convey an impression of abundance and richness. If you run out of wall space, utilize other surfaces – for example, tables, or the side of the staircase, if your collection is in a hall. If you are likely to continue adding to your collection for a long time to come, it might be a good idea to put it in a room where it will have space to spread – perhaps in a spare room, where its individuality may be a much appreciated asset and will compensate for a possible lack of atmosphere in a room not in constant use.

Photographs are natural candidates for any collection. These look better the closer they are set

▲
The pictures and photographs that make up this collection are arranged within well-defined vertical lines. Brighter mounts and frames act as a border, enlivening and unifying the composition. The collection is anchored from beneath by two unusual wood frames each containing a set of Edwardian photographs.

◀ A bright, busy background unifies this collection of historical memorabilia which spills over onto a similarly-covered table. A barometer and a large portrait anchor and unify the smaller elements.

▲
The bird's-eye maple wood frames of this collection are in harmony with the carved antique chairs carefully positioned beneath so that they form two groups that complement rather than compete with one another.

◀ A family tree of photos is set into an elegant wood screen for a movable display. Each panel has an identical arrangement but monotony is avoided by introducing three round portraits at eye level to the centre of each group.

▲ A variety of theatrical poses unites these photos, identically mounted and framed and hung in a veritable four-deep chorus line. Four central pictures arranged in a cross shape provide a focal point for this vast collection.

A black and white statement on the wall echoes the chequerboard floor. Unobtrusive picture-lights focus on individual works, while a picture on a music stand brings the collection into the room. ▶

▲ Collections of photographs often successfully encompass different periods, particularly when they portray family members, as with this group, hung close together to reinforce their relationship.

The subdued tones of the ▶ pictures on the wall leave the limelight to the free-standing photos and miniatures beneath. The smaller portraits stand in front with just enough of the back row revealed to solicit a closer look.

together. They need not be separately framed: many, particularly those that have some kind of emotional link, look good in a single large mount with several windows. Period and modern photographs can be combined but usually work best together where there is a constant theme such as family or place. You can also mix colour and black and white pictures within a collection, provided that the colours are not so bright that they overwhelm more subdued sepia or black and white tones.

The pictures that comprise a collection do not have to be hung inside a safe, rectangular arrangement: almost any shape will do. It is, as always, a question of balance. If you have one large and heavy painting within the group and nothing of equal weight to complement it, then redress the imbalance with two or more smaller pictures whose combined visual weight will give them equal strength.

Don't be afraid to mix different styles and shapes of frame within one display – a style that might clash in a small arrangement of three or four pictures may take its place more comfortably in a large, heterogenous group.

If you are just beginning to collect and have only a few items so far, consider hanging two or three different themes near each other until each group is full enough to stand alone. Or you may find a second theme to complement the main arrangement – for example, scatter some Japanese fans among a group of Oriental paintings. If the collection is still a little sparse, don't be tempted to try and fill the wall by spreading the pictures thinly, or you will lose the impression of abundance and completeness so intrinsic to a really good display.

Of all the historic approaches to picture hanging, one of the most pleasing conventions is that of the print room.

The art of fine print making reached its peak in the 18th century. Collecting prints was a favourite pursuit of the cognoscenti, and many of the larger English houses at this time had a room solely devoted to the display of prints.

Instead of framing the prints in the conventional manner, and then attaching them with chains or ribbons, the prints were pasted to the walls, which were often subsequently varnished over to protect the images on show.

Bows, rosettes and medallions might be hung over each print. The pictures were linked in columns and rows with an often very elaborate arrangement of ropes, tassels and ribbons. Each column might be crowned with elaborate swags of fruit and foliage. This arrangement of hanging devices became as much a part of the overall design as the prints themselves.

There are very few of these original rooms left. However, the print room is a concept that can easily be adapted by home owners today. Prints of all kinds are readily available, and can be found at every price level — although if you are going to varnish the prints directly to the wall, it is best to choose examples that are inexpensive.

An alternative idea is to imitate the general arrangement of the print room using conventional styles of framing and hanging. Instead of prints you could use paintings, posters or photographs. You can either use real ribbons, swags or rosettes or mimic their effect by stencilling, pasting down paper motifs (now made specially for the purpose) or even painting freehand.

▲
An Etruscan red background and a magnificent painted urn help to give this modern print room its distinctive ambience. The pictures, all dating from the mid-18th to the early 19th centuries, include a French circular copper-plate engraving showing the painted cupola of the Salon de la Guerre, Paris. Given pride of place above the fireplace, this makes a fine centrepiece. The terracotta-coloured prints show designs from a lost collection of antique vases. Stencilled motifs have been used to link the pictures in vertical ranks and to contain them at top and bottom by a *trompe l'oeil* frieze and dado. The use of heavy matt black frames prevents the overall effect from being too fussy. Empire-style chairs add to the mood and reinforce the effect of symmetry.

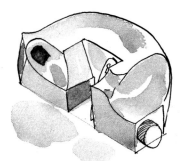

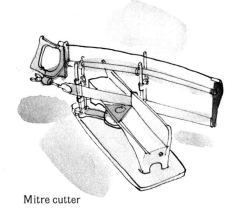

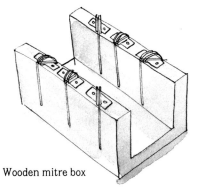

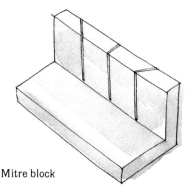

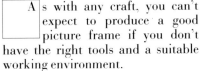

Mount cutter

Mitre cutter

Wooden mitre box

Mitre block

As with any craft, you can't expect to produce a good picture frame if you don't have the right tools and a suitable working environment.

If you don't have an ideal hobby workshop such as an extension to the house or a garage, you will have no option but to work in the house itself. Try to contrive things so that your work will not disrupt the rest of the household and that the rest of the household will not disrupt your work.

A kitchen table is likely to provide an adequate work surface, but its top should be protected with a sheet of plywood or chipboard with a layer of thick card on top — remember, you will be using sharp knives to cut mounts, and saws to cut frame mouldings, not to mention glues, stains and so on.

Think about the flooring, too. Cutting mouldings for frames will produce sawdust, so the flooring should have a smooth surface that can be swept easily. Glue and stains may drip on to the floor, so protect it with newspaper or a thick polythene sheet.

Another consideration is access — although even a relatively large picture frame is manageable, the length of moulding needed to make it is another matter entirely. Imagine a 2ft (60 cm) square frame — that's more than an 8 ft (2.75 m)

length of moulding. Would you be able to fit that into your work area? Would you be able to hold it on your work surface for cutting without it fouling a wall?

Tidiness and care while you are working are essential ingredients of success. Clear up after each operation, don't leave tools lying around when not in use, and keep any glues, paints or other liquids in sealed containers until needed, closing them again immediately after use.

Tools you will need

Always buy the best tools you can afford. Although the initial outlay may seem high, good-quality tools will last a lifetime if looked after, whereas cheaper versions will soon need replacing. Specialist framing tools are now available at reasonable prices and it is well worth investigating the possibilities at your local craft shop or framing supplier. Just how many special tools you buy will depend on how much framing you intend to do and how ambitious you are with regard to finishes. The following tools are essential:

Clear plastic rule To mark out mounts, inner backing boards and so on. It should be 2 ft (60 cm) long. The clear plastic type is more accurate for marking out precise measurements on mounts than a steel rule.

Craft knife or Stanley knife To cut mounts and inner backing cards. It should have replaceable blades.

Steel rule To guide the knife blade when cutting and for marking out frame lengths and so on.

Mount cutter A hand-held tool with an angled blade for cutting the bevelled edges of the mount's window.

Rasp To chamfer any rough edges on the backing board.

Mitre cutter This is a combination saw and mitre box (see below) designed to produce really accurate mitred ends to the lengths of frame moulding, so that when joined the corners of the frame make perfect right angles. It is the easiest way to achieve professional-quality joints.

Tenon or mitre saw Used together with a mitre box if you don't have a mitre cutter. Choose a fine-tooth version (24 teeth per inch/10 per cm) with a thin blade.

Mitre box or block To hold lengths of moulding while you cut their ends. At the very least, buy a good-quality hardwood one, but better still would be a metal version. The slots in inexpensive mitre boxes soon wear, leading to inaccurate cutting.

Hand or electric drill To drill pilot holes at the frame corners for reinforcing pins. You will also need a selection of very thin bits.

Corner clamps To hold the frame together while the glue hardens. The easiest type to use employs small corner brackets which are tensioned by a length of wire that runs around the entire frame. Otherwise you will need at least two separate G-clamps.

Pin hammer To drive in frame corner pins and pins to secure the backing board and other parts of the frame.

Nail punch To drive pin heads below the surface of the frame so that they can be hidden with filler.

G-clamps To hold moulding in a mitre box or the box itself to the work surface. They have many other clamping uses too.

Vice To hold sections of moulding while the corner reinforcing pins are added. It should be firmly clamped or bolted to the work surface and its jaws prevented from damaging the workpiece by gluing thin strips of wood to them.

Bradawl To make pilot holes for screws or for hanging fittings.

Plastic set square To check that frame joints are square and to mark out square cutting lines.

Pliers To remove reinforcing pins from the backs and corners of frames and for cutting picture frame wire.

Screwdriver To attach hanging plates and rings.

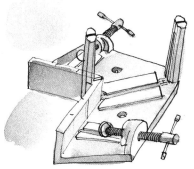
Metal mitre box

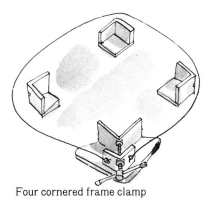
Four cornered frame clamp

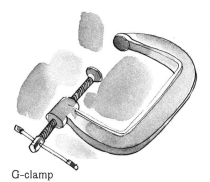
G-clamp

Pin hammer

Hanging fittings A selection of suitable fittings is shown on page 164.
Picture wire or nylon cord

Materials you will need
In addition to tools, you will need to provide yourself with the framing materials listed below:
Framer's moulding
Picture glass
Mount board
PVA wood glue
Panel pins (assorted sizes)
Wood filler For filling the holes in the frames.
Gummed paper tape For sealing the backs of frames.
Glass cleaner or methylated spirit
Acid-free paper tape For affixing the picture to the mount.

The more adventurous who are keen to decorate their mounts, cut their own glass or apply their own finishes to frames will also need to acquire some of the tools and materials listed below.
Glass cutter, T-square and **oilstone** or **emery cloth** if you want to cut your own glass. The best type of glass cutter is the oiled-wheel type, which is more expensive than the ordinary wheel type but is easier to use and will stay sharp longer.
Brushes Various brushes may be needed depending on the type of work you intend carrying out. Normal paint brushes up to about 1 in (2.5 cm) wide can be used to apply stain and some paints. Sable or ox-hair artists' brushes will be needed for applying colour washes to mounts. You will also need good nylon brushes for fine finishing work on frames. In addition, there are many special brushes for producing grained, stippled and marbled effects.
Ruling pen For adding ink lines around the window in the mount or to outline colour washes. The ruling pen has an adjustable nib for drawing lines of varying widths.
White spirit
Wallpaper paste or **water-based glue** For wet mounting.
Steel wool
Dry mounting film or **aerosol adhesive**
Shellac lacquer
Glass paper
Water-based paints For example, poster paints.
Wire wool
Knotting and **white primer** For preparing pine frames for finishing.

For decorating mounts you will need the following:
Watercolour paints For wash lines.
Gold paints For gold lines.
Gold gummed paper and **marbled paper** For use in strip form on the mount borders.

Parts of a frame
A frame may be made up of all or some of the parts described below: the details may vary to suit the type of picture being displayed.

Moulding The outer frame is made from wood or metal moulding, and there is a wide range of pre-finished and unfinished mouldings to choose from. The moulding incorporates a rabbet (or rebate) around the back into which the mount, artwork, backing card and backing board are fixed. Although frame mouldings can be made at home by gluing together lengths of standard woodworking mouldings, there are so many types specifically for picture framing that there is little point in attempting the job yourself.
Glass Not needed for oils but watercolours, prints and drawings are normally glazed. You may prefer to have your glass cut to size by the supplier rather than attempt this yourself. Either way, it should be ($\frac{1}{16}$ in) 2 mm thick. Non-reflective glass is available but is expensive and its textured surface may obscure the finer detail of the artwork, particularly if there is any gap between the artwork and the glass – for example, because of a mount.
Mount For watercolours, prints, drawings, photographs and pastels. Not normally used with oils. Mount boards have a coloured surface and a white core so that when the window for the picture is cut, the white will act as an outline for the artwork. A range of colours is available, but mounts can also be covered with coloured papers, fabrics and so on. Boards come in various thicknesses, the most common being 4-sheet, 6-sheet and 8-sheet. If a thicker board is required, two sheets can be glued together. It is advisable to use **conservation board** when making a mount for any original work, and for anything of value this is essential. Conservation board is acid-free and will not cause discoloration of the picture: this can occur with ordinary boards, which deteriorate quite quickly.
Backing card A piece of mount board which supports the artwork. Again, conservation board must be used if the work has any value.
Backing board The outer protective backing of the picture – usually made from thick card or hardboard. The latter is by far the best.
Hanging fittings To attach the picture to the wall. There is a wide range of hanging fittings to choose from, depending on the type and size of frame. They range from simple screw eyes to substantial rings and metal plates. In most cases, brass picture wire or nylon picture cord is stretched between a pair of fittings.

If your artwork is to be displayed with a mount, you should cut this before making the frame. Although it is true that it would be easier to adjust the size of the mount to fit the frame than vice versa, the important thing is to display the artwork in the best possible manner, and that means having a mount of the right size.

Before deciding on the size of mount, however, you will have to work out just how much of the artwork you want to show, unless you intend displaying the entire image. One simple way of doing this is to cut two L-shaped pieces of card and place them over opposite corners of the picture so that they form a frame shape: by moving the cards in and out and up and down, you will soon see just how much you want to show. Note down the size of the window; then decide on the width of the mount borders. Between 2–3 in (5–7.5 cm) is the usual width of the mount border unless the picture is very large (28 x 24 in/70 x 60 cm or over). Remember that for the sake of balance you should make the space at the bottom of the picture slightly larger than that at the top (see page 16).

Cutting the mount to size
It is important that your mount is cut square, that is, with the corners at exact right angles. Otherwise, it will not fit your frame properly and the window will not be centred. With this in mind, don't assume that your new sheet of mount board *is* square. Use your set square to check it and if necessary re-cut an end to get an exact right-angled corner. Working from this corner, mark out the height and width of your mount, using the plastic rule, and then draw the outside dimensions of the mount. Do all the marking and cutting out from the reverse side of the board so that any accidental marks or mistakes will not be seen.

Lay the card face down on a sheet of cheap, thick card placed on a suitable cutting board. Then, holding the steel straight edge firmly down with one hand as a guide for the knife blade (with the vertical edge, never the bevelled edge, against the line) cut along the pencil lines with a firm, smooth movement. Try to make the cut with one pass — if your blade is razor sharp (which it needs to be) this should not be a problem. However, if the card is thick and one stroke not sufficient, carefully go over the line again, taking care not to let the blade wander. Use a set square to check the measurements and ensure that the corners are square.

Cutting the window
Marking out the window on the backing card is easy: let us assume that you have decided on borders of 2 ¾ in (7 cm) at the top and sides and 3 in (7.5 cm) at the bottom. Lay the plastic ruler across the mount at the bottom and mark off 2¾ in (7 cm) from the left- and right-hand sides. Repeat this at the top and then join up the marks with two pencil lines drawn against a plastic ruler so as to give you the sides of your window. Then measure out the bottom and top lines in the same way, working from the bottom upward, remembering the bottom border is 3 in (7.5 cm).

The edge of the window should be bevelled, at an angle of about 60°. This not only prevents shadows from being thrown on to the picture, but also helps draw the eye to it. Cutting this bevel with a Stanley knife is difficult. Cut the mount card to size along the straight side of

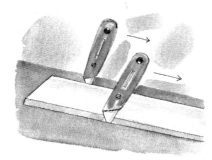

Cutting the window

the straight edge; for the window, cut against the bevelled side, holding the knife in your fist. By far the best way of doing the job is to use a hand-held mount cutter which has its blade set at the correct angle and is adjustable to accommodate differing thicknesses of card. Some cutters come with an integral steel rule as a guide, in which case follow the manufacturer's instructions for cutting. Most, however, are designed to be used with a metal straight edge as a guide. Place the mount card face down on the cutting board and insert the blade of the cutter at the bottom left-hand corner of the window.

Place the straight edge against the left-hand edge of the cutter and align it using the ruler so that it is equidistant from the pencil line along its entire length. Holding the straight edge firmly down, push the cutter along it with a steady pressure until you have cut a fraction beyond the line which crosses it at the top of the window. Remove the cutter. Turn the mount 90° and repeat for the next cut. Continue until you have made all four cuts, at which point the centre should drop neatly out. This will take practice, however, and until you have learned to judge the correct point at which to start and finish each cut you will need to cut through at the corners with a sharp knife to free the centre.

Oval or round windows are much more difficult to cut, although if you have a bevel cutter you could make a stiff cardboard template and run the cutter around this. In the main, however, it is probably better to buy mounts with such windows ready made.

Using a mount cutter

Mounting the artwork
Cut a piece of backing card to the same outside measurements as the mount itself. (If the artwork is on substantial paper, however, and is the same size as the mount, all that may be necessary is to assemble it with the mount in the frame.)

Making a hinge mount
In a hinge mount, the artwork is sandwiched between a backing card and a window mount which are hinged together. If you later want to replace the picture with one of a similar size, you could simply slide the old picture out and position the new one in its place. Lay the mount face down on the cutting board. Butt the backing card against the top edge of the mount and join the two with a strip of gummed paper. Fold the back over and press down on the resultant hinge to secure it. You now have your hinge mount. Put this down on the cutting board face upwards and open it. Place the artwork on the backing card and close the mount over it. By moving

the artwork about gently you can establish it in the correct position inside the window. The next step is to attach the artwork. The correct way to do this is to stick two short strips of gummed acid-free paper tape (never clear or masking tape) to the back of the artwork so that they project above its top edge. Then stick these projecting tabs down on the backing card by pressing short lengths of gummed tape over them. Securing only the top edge in this manner allows the artwork to expand and contract with atmospheric conditions without fear of wrinkling. And the gummed tape is easily removed by dampening it with water should you wish to replace or reframe the artwork at some later date.

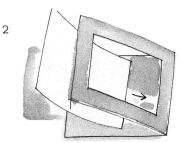

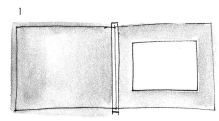

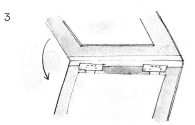

Making a hinge mount

Wet mounting

There are two other methods (wet and dry) of mounting the artwork to a backing card, but they should never be used with any original piece of work as they can cause damage to the artwork in the long run and may affect its value.

Wet mounting simply means using glue, wallpaper paste or some other water-based glue, and a backing card of at least 6-sheet thickness to prevent warping. These glues need to be used with care to prevent bubbles from appearing. Apply the glue thinly and evenly to the backing card with a brush and lay the artwork down onto it. Place a clean sheet of tissue paper against it and press it down with a soft cloth, working from the centre outwards. This can be quite difficult, and it is best to practise first with scrap materials until you get the hang of it. Don't use a water-based adhesive on any artwork that might run if dampened or on artwork on thin paper.

The same procedure can be carried out using an aerosol adhesive, which has the advantage that the artwork can be lifted and repositioned before it finally dries, allowing bubbles and creases to be teased out.

Dry mounting

The professional method of dry mounting is to use a special adhesive sheet that is placed between the artwork and backing and fused to both in a heated press. This is the best way to block-mount photographs and posters on chipboard panels.

You should be able to obtain these adhesive sheets from good art shops or framers' suppliers. You can then use an iron heated to the correct temperature for silks or synthetics to apply the heat necessary to fuse the adhesive. Protective paper sheets are supplied with the adhesive sheets to prevent damage to the artwork. Clean the picture carefully to remove dust and specks of dirt, then turn it over onto a clean, dry surface and lay an adhesive sheet over the back of the artwork. Gently place the tip of the warm iron over the centre of the adhesive sheet, so that it is lightly attached to the artwork. Trim the excess adhesive sheet to the same size as the picture, using a sharp knife drawn carefully against a steel rule. Lay the print face up on the backing card and pass the iron over

Dry mounting

two opposite corners of the adhesive sheet (lifting first one corner, then the other) to attach it to the backing board. Cover the picture with the protective sheet provided and iron over its surface working outwards from the centre. Leave the mounted picture to cool and then trim any excess adhesive sheet.

If you are using a window mount and have wet- or dry-mounted your picture, you can affix the mounted work to the back of the window mount with gummed tape. In this case, there is no need to make a hinge mount.

Decorating the mount

If you want something more elaborate than a simple, single-colour mount, there are various ways in which a more decorative effect can be achieved.

Multiple mounts

Double or even triple mounts of different colours can be used so that the artwork is bordered by coloured bands. In this case it is vital that each window is cut square. Cut the mount cards to size in the usual way. Then cut the window of the inside mount as normal but keeping the cutout middle section by you. Mark out the second mount with a slightly narrower border, allowing, say ¼ in (0.5 cm) less all around. Lay the scrap section from the first mount against your second mount window and check that the difference in size is even all the way around. Variations can be corrected by redrawing the lines of the second window before cutting it. Stick the two together using the wet-mounting method, aerosol glue or double-sided adhesive tape. For a triple mount, repeat the procedure, reducing the border by a further ¼ in (0.5 cm) all round. This time use the cutout from the second mount to check the measurements of the third window.

Wash lines and decorated borders

With practice a variety of decorative effects can be obtained using watercolour wash line borders, either on their own or combined with strips of gold or decorative papers (see pages 54-5). Try a simple wash line first. Draw in the outline of the border in very faint pencil lines measuring from the window opening with the plastic rule. Prepare the watercolour that you intend to use, following the manufacturer's instructions. Using a brush that is the same, or nearly the same, width as the band, moisten the area within the band with fresh, clean water. This will prevent the paint from becoming patchy when it is applied. Shake the excess water from the brush. Charge it with the watercolour and apply it to the first side of the washed band in one continuous sweep. Then apply the watercolour to the other three sides. Several layers of watercolour usually give a better effect than one thick one. Again, practise on scrap mounts until you are satisfied with the results. The main problem will occur at the corners and only with practice will you achieve the necessary speed to avoid leaving darker patches at the joins.

Allow the border to dry, then add the edging lines in watercolour or ink with a ruling pen guided by a steel rule held bevelled edge downward to prevent the ink from smudging. Try to make each line in one movement without having to recharge the pen, otherwise the breaks may show.

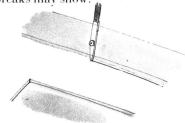

Using a ruling pen

More elaborate borders can then be achieved by adding additional lines on the inside and outside of the wash line and by combining a narrow inner border with a wider outside border in another, complementary colour. A full wash border is not always essential and a quieter effect can be achieved by simply applying one or two ink or watercolour lines.

The mount may also be embellished by using decorative paper, either on its own or bordered by ink or watercolour lines, or in conjunction with a wash line. The simplest is gummed gold (or silver) paper which comes in sheet form from which you cut narrow strips, usually about ⅛ in (3 mm) wide, as needed. Again, mark out the guidelines in faint pencil and stick down the gold paper between them, overlapping the corners and then cutting through them to form mitred joints. Or use strips of marbled or other decorative paper, sticking them down with double-sided tape. You could also use watercolour to paint the white bevel around the window.

Covering a mount

If you cannot obtain mounting card or pre-cut mounts in the colour you want, or if you plan to coordinate your picture collection with an overall colour scheme, one of the simplest solutions is to cover the mounts yourself using coloured art paper, wallpaper or fabric. This allows you to achieve the precise effect you want and to display your pictures in a unique way; it can also work out cheaper than buying pre-cut mounts, especially for larger pictures.

You can buy suitable paper from art shops in a huge range of colours and finishes, ranging from delicate moiré and marbled effects to imitation leather and metallic foil. If you prefer to use wallpaper or fabrics, you can use offcuts from your own decorating jobs or even ask in decorating and furnishing stores for out-of-date pattern books (ideal for small prints) or leftovers from batches or rolls.

Apart from the covering material

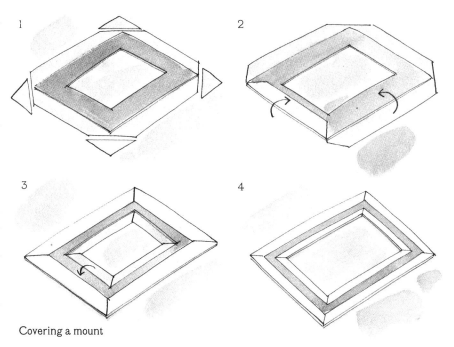

1 2 3 4

Covering a mount

itself you will still need some card to make the actual mounts. If the material you have chosen is thin and will follow the mitred edges of the window easily, it's best to use ordinary white mounting card. However, with thicker fabrics there is no point in cutting mitres – a square-edged window will look just as good – and you can use any suitable thick card.

With thin materials, you can tackle the covering in one or two ways. If you want to have a white contrasting mitred edge to the window, stick the paper or fabric to the face of the mount first, and then cut the window in the usual way with a sharp knife or a proprietary cutting tool so the core of the card is left exposed. If, however, you want the material to cover the edges of the window as well, cut the window with mitred edges first and then lay the mount on the rear face of the covering material so that you can cut it and fold the tongues over onto the rear face of the mount. With this method, it may not be necessary to use adhesive on the face of the mount if you draw the covering material tightly over the edges of the window and the outside edges of the mount before sticking it down. Use this cut-and-fold technique with thicker fabric covers too, but don't bother to mitre the window edges.

You need to be careful when using an adhesive to cover a mount, as water-based adhesives may cause the material to wrinkle or the colours to run. One of the easiest types to use is a solvent-based aerosol adhesive, which can be sprayed onto the face of the mount before it is laid onto the covering material. It is available from art suppliers and commercial stationers. This type of adhesive provides enough tack to hold the covering material in place on the mount yet also allows the bond to be separated and remade if necessary.

Having prepared the mount and inner backing board, you can turn your attention to the frame itself, choosing a suitable pre-finished or unfinished picture frame moulding (see Framer's Portfolio section, pages 50-89). If you are framing an oil painting that has no mount or perhaps a piece of needlework which is also likely to be mounted on stretchers, the first job is to check whether it is square — there is a good chance that it won't be. An easy way to do this is to measure from corner to corner diagonally. If the artwork is square, the diagonal measurements will be the same; if they differ, the artwork is out of square.

You should, of course, make sure that the moulding you choose has a rabbet (the groove or recess along the moulding into which the picture, mount and glass will be slotted) that is wide enough to cover the required amount of the picture edge. If the picture is out of square, you should also take this into account and choose a moulding with a rabbet wide enough to conceal the problem. If the rabbet is narrow you may end up showing parts of the artwork that you would prefer to conceal.

Calculating the moulding length

There are various methods for calculating the amount of moulding needed for a picture frame, but however you come by the answer, remember to make allowance for cutting. If you buy a piece of moulding that is exactly the required length, by the time you have cut it into four pieces it is bound to be a little too short. Add on a good couple of inches to the final calculation, or round the figure up to the nearest foot to be safe.

Probably the simplest method of working out how much moulding you need is to measure the length and width of the artwork or mount if any, and then add ⅛ in (3 mm) to each measurement as an allowance for fitting. Without this, you might find the artwork too snug a fit in the finished frame. Add the two measurements together and multiply them by two to give you the total length of the artwork's perimeter. If the artwork is out of square, measure all four sides in turn and base your calculations on the longest of each pair of sides.

Next you must allow for the fact that the moulding projects beyond the artwork at the corners, and for this you need to know the width of the moulding. Multiply this by eight and add the result to the artwork's perimeter length. You now have the total amount of moulding required, but don't forget to add on the allowance for cutting.

Whenever possible, buy the moulding in one length rather than two in case any manufacturing inaccuracies have caused variations in width which will be very obvious in the completed frame. You can, of course, get the supplier to cut the piece exactly in half if it is too unwieldy to carry home. For a really large frame, you may have no alternative but to buy two separate pieces, in which case compare them very carefully, particularly the face width. Check, too, that the length of moulding is straight by looking along it — reject any that is bent or twisted.

Cutting the moulding

When marking and cutting the moulding, work on one piece at a time rather than attempting to mark out the entire length in one go. The first job is to trim one edge of the moulding to a mitre running in the right direction.

Lay the moulding in the mitre box so that the rabbeted edge is up against the far side of the box with its bottom flat against the base of the box. The end should be about ¼ in (5 mm) beyond the saw slot in the far edge. Cut down through the face of the moulding so that any splintering that occurs when the saw blade breaks through will be on the back. Hold the moulding firmly in place with your free hand or a G-clamp (placing a piece of scrap wood beneath the cramp shoe to give protection to the moulding) and cut the end to a mitre with the tenon saw or mitre cutter. Saw slowly and let the weight of the saw do the cutting rather than forcing it, which will damage the wood.

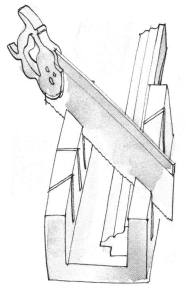

Cutting the first moulding

From the cut end, measure out the required length of the first side of the frame along the outside edge — that is, measure the length (or height) of the artwork plus the ⅛ in (3 mm) fitting allowance plus twice the moulding width. Mark it in

pencil and return to the mitre box, aligning the pencil mark with the slot in the box. This time the mitre will run in the opposite direction so use the appropriate slot.

Having cut the first length, you will need to trim the end of the main piece of moulding again so that the mitre runs in the right direction. Again, leave about ¼ in (5 mm) from the end. Make the cut and remove a triangular section of wood. Now hold the first length against the moulding and align the ends, using the first piece as a guide for marking the length of the

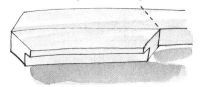

Marking the second moulding

second. Cut this out in the same way. Then cut the third and fourth pieces, measuring out the first of these and using it as a guide for marking out the last. Although the sawn ends may have rough edges, never sand them, as you are bound to round them slightly and then they will never fit together properly. Any rough edges can be cleaned up with fine glasspaper, but it is better to leave these until the frame has been assembled in case you make the mitred joint uneven.

Clamping and gluing the frame

You can glue and pin the sides of the frame using a vice as an aid. However, this is not easy as you would need to hold one freshly glued piece against another while driving in a panel pin, and there is a tendency for the glue to make them slide apart. You would then have to allow for this by offsetting the end of one against the other, but it is difficult to judge just how much of an offset to allow. Therefore, by far the easiest and surest way of assembling the frame is with frame clamps.

The best type of clamp has three L-shaped corner brackets and a fourth adjustable bracket with wire running around all four. Apply PVA wood glue to the ends of the frame mouldings and place them in the corner brackets. Fit the wire around the outside, making sure it is located in the notches in the brackets, and tension it by tightening the screws of the adjustable bracket. This will ensure a firm, even pressure all round and will hold the frame square while the glue hardens.

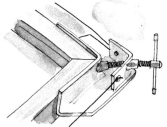

Clamping the frame

If you are using two mitre clamps, assemble the two pairs of adjacent sides to form L-shapes. Insert the lengths of moulding in the clamp, arranging them so that they meet exactly at a right angle and tighten the screws. If the mouldings you are using are soft or have a delicate finish, place pieces of scrap wood between the shoes and the mouldings to protect the wood. Then release one screw, slide the moulding back and apply glue to the ends of both mouldings. Bring them back together and tighten the slackened screw. Any glue that oozes from the joint should be wiped off immediately with a damp cloth. When the glue holding the first two joints

has hardened, clamp and glue the two L-shaped pairs of mouldings together to make a complete frame.

Drilling and pinning the corners
For added strength, each corner of the frame should be reinforced with two panel pins unless the moulding is too narrow to accommodate more than one pin. Although these can be driven straight into the wood, it is better to drill narrow pilot holes first to prevent the ends of the moulding splitting. Make the holes slightly smaller in diameter than the pins themselves. Although the shape of the corner clamps may allow the holes to be drilled and the pins hammered in while the mouldings are still in the clamps, it is safer to remove the frame when the glue has hardened and clamp one length in a vice while drilling through the adjacent piece.

The length of the pins should be about double the width of the moulding. They should be driven in at a slight angle to each other (see diagram). Drive them down below the surface of the moulding with a nail punch and fill the resulting depressions with wood filler. Even in a pre-finished frame, the spots of filler can be disguised with paint spots. If you apply these with a brush that has a fine enough tip, they will be so small that any slight mismatch in colour will not be noticed.

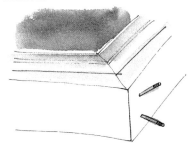

Driving in panel pins

Metal frames are quite popular for displaying prints, posters and photographs. The slim sections give a clean, modern look and will fit in with a wide variety of decorative schemes. There are two basic types: the all-metal extrusion and a metal-covered wood moulding complete with rabbet. In both cases, the metal is aluminium which comes in a variety of coloured finishes, with either a highly polished surface or a subdued satin finish. The method of assembly varies with the moulding type. The extrusion type comes in kits of ready-cut, matching sides in various lengths. To make up a frame, two kits of the correct length must be purchased.

Assembling a metal kit frame
Because the aluminium extrusions are supplied in set lengths, to a certain extent you are limited in your choice of frame dimensions and you may have to compromise. For example, you may have to trim the edges of the print or poster slightly to fit the nearest suitable size – or use a wide mount to make up space. The glass and backing board should be sized according to the extrusion lengths. The glass can then be laid on top of the print or poster, which will serve as a cutting guide.

To assemble the frame, put together three sides, joining them with the L-shaped brackets provided. The precise method of fastening the brackets varies from kit to kit and you should follow the manufacturer's instructions. Next, slide the glass, mount (if any), artwork and backing board into the groove around the inside of the frame, making sure they are seated properly at the bottom. The fourth side is slotted over the glass and

secured with the remaining two L-shaped brackets. In most cases, spring clips are provided to fit between the backing board and extrusions to hold the glass, artwork and mount firmly in place.

Hangers are supplied with some kits and are usually inserted into a slot in the back of the side extrusions and then turned to lock them into place. If no hangers are provided, you will need to attach ring fittings to the backing board with bifurcated rivets.

Metal-covered wood moulding
One of the problems with metal-covered wood moulding is in cutting the material – you need a hacksaw and, ideally, a metal mitre box, although the pieces are actually assembled into a frame in much the same way as normal moulding. The ends should be mitred and can be glued together with PVA wood glue while the mouldings are held in corner clamps. As panel pins driven into the sides of the frame to reinforce the corners would be obtrusive, it is best to drive them in from the bottom and top of each corner rather than from the sides, so that they are not visible (see diagram).

Normal hanging fittings can be used, screwed into the back of the moulding as with a normal frame.

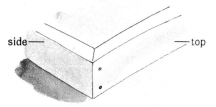

side——   ——top

Positioning the panel pins

There are many variations on the simple wooden frame. Some popular examples are given over the following two pages.

Wide-margin and slip frames

Wide-margin frame mouldings incorporate a broad, flat strip in the centre which offers many decorative possibilities for the frame itself. The strip can be treated with a colour that blends or contrasts with the rest of the frame, or alternatively it could be covered with a fabric such as hessian.

Wide-margin frame

With care, wide-margin mouldings can be made by gluing a simple flat batten between two proprietary mouldings. These should be assembled in one long strip before cutting out the four individual sides for the frame. Hold the mouldings together with G-clamps while the glue hardens. Once the new wide-margin moulding has been made, it can be cut and assembled in the same manner as a simpler moulding.

Slip frames fit inside conventional frames and may be used to provide an added decorative aspect to the frame when fitted in front of the glass, or to provide a little extra space between the glass and the item being displayed when fitted behind it – useful where you are framing a pastel without a mount or, alternatively, a collage. Slip frames normally come in quite thin sections and may already be finished in gold or silver or a fabric covering. However, any suitable wooden moulding may be used for a slip frame and finished to suit your taste. Make sure that the rabbet in the main frame moulding is deep enough to accommodate the slip together with the glass, artwork and other inserts.

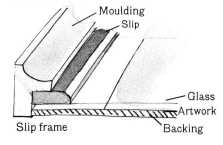

Slip frame

Slip mouldings should be cut to length with mitred ends to fit the finished outer frame. If you are careful when taking the measurements, they should fit snugly in place without any need for gluing together or pinning. If you have made them a bit loose, it would be better to glue them together and insert them as a complete, inner frame. If the slip moulding has a rabbet, make this up as a frame first, then cut the outer frame mouldings to fit round it.

Double-glass frames

If the item you want to display has something of interest on the reverse, you will need a double-glass frame. For something like a signature which doesn't need to be displayed but needs to be seen when necessary, a window can be cut in the backing board and the back of the frame either glazed completely or a piece of transparent plastic glued over the window. If you are using glass, choose a frame with a deep rabbet and use thicker glass ⅛ in (3 mm) on the back so that it does not crack when pinned in. Use smaller pins and drive them in gently as far as possible. Seal up with a narrow strip of gummed paper.

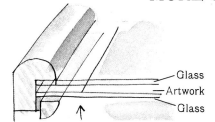

Double-glass frame

You may have a document or a piece of embroidery, that is of visual interest on both sides. This can be sandwiched between two sheets of glass sealed together with masking tape and held in a normal frame with turn buttons. This will allow you to alternate the side on view at will.

Freestanding frames

You can make a light kind of freestanding frame that is ideal for photographs and the like. Normally quite small and made of narrow moulding, it has a hinged strut at the back for support. The frame itself, together with the glass, mount, artwork and backing, is assembled in the normal manner. However, the backing board must be modified to incorporate the strut. You should be able to buy a ready-made hinged strut from your local framing supplier. Rather than pinning the backing board in place, use turn buttons, which will allow you to open the back at any time to change the picture.

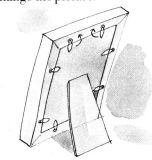

Freestanding frame

Box frames

When it comes to displaying bulky items such as jewelry, medals and so on, a deep frame is required to accommodate them. If the items are easily cleaned, you may prefer simply to make a deep, unglazed frame from a suitable moulding, pinning the backing board to the reverse face. However, if they need protecting from dust, the frame should be glazed to make, in effect, a miniature display case.

For this type of frame you need a moulding with a rabbet deep enough to give plenty of room between the glass and the backing board in order to accommodate the bulk of the items. Assuming you have found a moulding with a deep enough rabbet, the first job is to assemble it into a frame as normal.

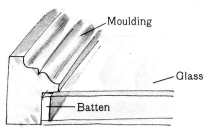

Box frame with rabbet

Add the glass, then cut thin spacer battens to size with mitred ends to fit around the inside of the frame and separate the glass from the backing board. Cut the battens as tight as possible so that there is no need to glue or pin them together. They should be narrow enough to leave a rabbet at the back of the frame for fitting the backing. Depending on the item being displayed, you can either mount it on an inner backing card and fit a backing board as well or mount the item directly to the outer backing board. This should be secured to the back of the frame in the normal manner.

If you can't find a moulding with a deep enough rabbet, you can use a standard picture frame moulding extended by gluing and nailing square moulding to the back.

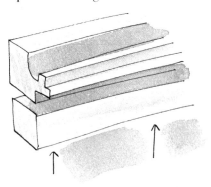

Extended frame moulding

Frames of this type are most effective if the backing is covered in a material such as velvet and the spacer battens either covered in the same material or painted or stained a dark colour so that they "disappear". Mounting the object may require ingenuity depending on what it is. Often small holes can be drilled through the backing and fine wire, thread or nylon fishing line used to hold the object in place. Whatever the method chosen, take pains to keep it as unobtrusive as possible.

You will need to mount the box frame in such a way that it is flat against the wall. To do this, fit flush-mounting picture plates to the top edge or to the sides and drive screws through these into the wall, having first drilled and plugged the holes if necessary.

Clip frames

With clip frames, the artwork is mounted on a sheet of hardboard or chipboard (about ¾ in/2 cm thick) and a sheet of glass clipped to the front. This is an ideal method for displaying posters and prints, but should not be used for anything that might be damaged by dust.

It is essential that the edges of the board are straight and that it is cut square, otherwise the finished appearance will be spoiled. The glass should be cut to the same size as the board and its sharp edges must be smoothed by rubbing with an oilstone or emery cloth. Both board and glass should normally be the same size as the poster, but if the poster has a wide border that can be trimmed the board and glass can be smaller. In this case, lay the glass on the poster and use as a trimming guide.

If you are using hardboard as a backing, you can hold it to the glass with spring clips. These have short tails that fit into holes drilled in the back of the board and then clip over the edge of the board and glass. To protect the back of the artwork from the tails, mount it on a thin sheet of card. Use D-ring hanging fittings attached to the back of the hardboard. Don't try to attach the wire to the clips as you are likely to

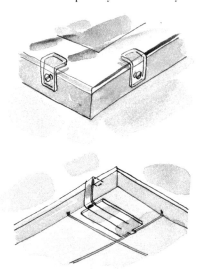

Two examples of clip frames

pull them loose and break the glass.

In the case of chipboard, the glass is held to the board with small metal or plastic mirror clips which are screwed to the edges with proper chipboard screws. To provide the chipboard backing with more presentable edges, you can trim it with masking tape or black insulating tape. Again, it is wise to mount the artwork on thin card to protect it from any unevenness in the backing board. To hang a frame of this kind, fix D-rings to the back with chipboard screws.

Your local glass supplier will cut the glass to the correct size for your frame, and you may prefer to opt for this solution, particularly if a large piece is required. However, there is no reason why you should not glaze a picture yourself, provided that you take a lot of care and approach the job with confidence. Remember, newly cut glass has extremely sharp edges, so always handle it with caution.

Cutting glass is not difficult but it does require the correct technique so it is a good idea to practise on some small pieces of scrap glass first. Use glass that is 1/16 in (2 mm) thick (known as 18 oz glass). You can choose between reflective and non-reflective, but the latter is much more expensive and may actually obscure some of the finer detail of your artwork.

Accurate measurement is essential – if your piece of glass is a fraction of an inch too large, you will have to start again. Always include a 1/8 in (3 mm) clearance on the width and height as a fitting allowance.

You will need a flat work surface at least as large all round as the sheet of glass you will be cutting, and preferably larger. Cover it with several sheets of newspaper or an old blanket to cushion the glass. You can mark out the piece to be cut with a felt-tip pen, but it would be better to use a wax pencil which won't smudge easily. Your cutting line should run from one edge of the glass right across to the other – you can't make sharp changes in direction.

You will also need a glass cutter, and a steel or wooden straight edge or T-square to guide it. The best glass cutter to buy is the oiled-wheel type. You should find this easier to use than the cheaper yet more readily available normal wheel cutter which will wear out quite quickly, and must be lubricated by dipping in cutting oil or white spirit regularly during cutting.

To make the cut, hold the straight edge to one side of the line and place the cutter against it so that the tip or wheel is exactly on your marked line. Hold the cutter like a pen. Then, applying a firm, steady pressure, draw the cutter from one edge of the glass to the other in one movement. In fact, the cutter scores the surface of the glass rather than cutting right through it and as it does so you will hear a steady crackling sound. As you practise, get used to the sound the cutter makes when it produces a good cut and try to reproduce it each time. Make only one stroke with the cutter: repeating it may cause the glass to break in the wrong place or damage the instrument.

To complete the cut, gently lift the glass enough to slide the straight edge underneath so that it is just to one side of the score mark. Press down on both sides of the line with your fingertips and the glass will snap cleanly in two. Finish off the cut edge by rubbing along it with an oilstone or an emery cloth, prefer-

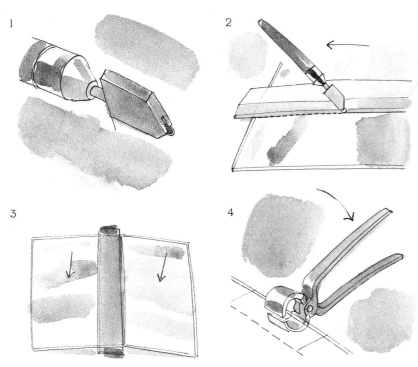

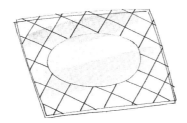

Cutting the glass

ably wrapped round a sanding block to avoid cutting your fingers.

If a very thin strip of glass must be removed, you can't use this method of snapping it, as in trying to do so you will probably break the whole sheet. Professionals use special wide-jawed glass pliers to break off the strip bit by bit along the line. In the absence of these, a pair of pincers can be used, but it is a good idea to score several cuts across the strip, so that it can be nibbled away a little at a time.

Cutting an oval or round piece of glass is more difficult, and you will need to make a cardboard template (slightly smaller than the size actually required) to run the cutter round. First cut the glass down to a rectangle that is just slightly larger than the template. Then lay the template on the glass and run the cutter firmly round it. Cross-hatch

the waste glass with the cutter and carefully nibble away the pieces with glass pliers or pincers until the correct shape is left. A special tool is also available for cutting circular pieces. It is used like a pair of compasses. having a cutter at the end of an adjustable arm that is held to the glass by a suction pad. To remove the circle, however, you would still need to nibble away the glass around it. Finally, sand the cut edge, as already described. working firmly but carefully.

Cutting a glass oval

The finish of the completed frame offers plenty of scope for a wide range of decorative techniques. You can either choose to enhance the natural grain of the wooden mouldings or use colour to emphasize their shape or produce interesting patterns and effects.

Simple stained finishes
Staining the wood will bring out the best in the grain, and you need not confine yourself to using traditional wood colours; there is a wide range of other tones to choose from. You will need to stain the moulding before it is cut into sections for the frame. In this way, the degree of staining will be uniform on all four pieces and you won't get a build-up of stain that will cause dark patches at the corners of the frame. First sand the moulding with fine glasspaper until it is smooth. Then wipe it clean with a cloth soaked in white spirit. Apply the stain evenly with a brush without going back to touch in pale patches – a second coat will always produce a darker finish. If there are any areas where you have spread it too thin, the rest of the moulding will have to be sanded until it appears the same colour. Then, if you wish, you can add a second coat.

A stained frame can be finished in various ways. A matt or semi-matt varnish will produce a hardwearing surface or you can obtain a softer finish by treating the stained wood with a good-quality furniture wax containing beeswax. Alternatively, brush on two coats of shellac, rubbing down each with steel wool, and then apply the wax. Various tinted waxes are also available, and they can be used to produce interesting effects on both stained and painted surfaces.

Simple painted finishes
If you decide to paint your frame there are endless combinations of colours and finishes to choose from. Oil-based paints, acrylics and water-based emulsions are all suitable finishes.

Easiest of all is to paint the frame a single solid colour. A more unusual idea is to paint the frame in two or more colours, using the contours of the mouldings as your guide. A deep, rich tone on the outer and inner edges, for example, might have a lighter tone of the same colour in the central panel. Alternatively, you could take a tone from the picture for the centre of the frame, and surround that with a colour that creates a gentle contrast.

Masking tape allows all sorts of easy effects with paint. The corners of the frame can be masked and then painted in contrast to the rest of the frame. Or use the masking tape to make chunky stripes around the perimeter.

Whatever type of paint finish you choose, the frame must be sanded well beforehand so that it is perfectly smooth, and treated with wood primer to seal the grain. If the moulding is of pine, treat it with knotting first. After priming, paint the frame with an undercoat suitable for the type of paint finish you will be using. When each painted coat has dried, sand it down carefully using the finest glasspaper you can buy, before applying the next coat. Make sure your brushes are of good quality, clean and free from loose bristles.

One of the most effective and simple paint treatments is to paint the frame with a white undercoat and then apply a very thin coat of diluted colour over the top. This will give a translucent quality to the finish, the white undercoat showing through the top coat. Water-based paints are ideal for this, and you can mix your own colours by adding artists' powder paints to ordinary white emulsion and then thinning them with water.

Special finishes

Simple stained or painted finishes are the easiest techniques to use on picture frames, but there are several more complex finishes which, although they require a degree of artistic skill and colour sense, can be achieved with practice. These finishes are especially suitable as ways to add distinction to a decorative print. None of them demands any specialized equipment.

You can get some quite interesting effects with simple versions of spattering and sponging. To spatter successfully you need a stiff brush whose bristles have been cut down nearly to the base, a firm hand, and a good eye for colour. Paint the base coat either white (or ivory) or a dark colour, and allow to dry. Then taking either a dark shade if you are using a pale base, or a lighter tone if you have a deep-toned base, dip the brush in the paint and spatter it across the surface. Masking tape can be used here too – to mask corners, for example, and then spatter them in a darker or lighter shade.

Spattering

Sponging is another easy and attractive finish. The best tool is a marine sponge – the size of the sponge will determine the shape of the markings. Use a fairly small sponge as too big a marking could merely look blotchy rather than artistic.

Again, paint the base colour – usually a light one for sponging – and then when the base coat is dry apply the sponge colour. Either sponge *off* – painting the colour on quickly, and then removing as much or as little as you like with the sponge; or sponge *on* – applying the second colour directly to the frame with the sponge.

Stencilling is another technique

Sponging

which you can do yourself. Choose from a huge range of readily available stencil designs or cut out your own. If you are making your own try and find the sheets of tough transparent film (Melanex) sold in speciality art shops. These allow you to trace a motif more easily than you could do with the traditional stencil card. Use a china writing pencil (chinagraph) and then cut out the pieces with a scalpel. Remember to fasten the decal securely to the frame. Work in sections so that the decal does not slip, and to ensure that you are getting your stencil design in the right place. The design can be as plain or as intricate as you wish, but

the simplest designs are often the most successful, such as those favoured by the early American settlers who used stencilling on their floors, walls and woodwork.

Stencilling

You could invent your own finishes, adapting techniques you have already tried, and devising new ones for yourself. Remember that with a bit of artistic flair and some determined experimentation with colours and design, it is often possible to achieve a far more interesting finish than many ready-finished frames could offer. It is possible to do your own gilding if you wish, but the cost of the gold leaf is so high, the leaves themselves so fragile and so difficult to attach correctly to the frame, that unless you are very sure of your own skill it is one of the finishing techniques best left to a professional.

Before you assemble the frame, glass, artwork and so on, try each piece separately in the frame first as a double check that everything will fit. If you are glazing the frame, make sure that the glass is perfectly clean on the inside face and that any mount and the artwork itself are free from specks of dirt and dust before you begin to assemble everything: once the backing board is in place and sealed, you won't want to pull it all

apart again.

Assemble the backing board, backing card, artwork and mount. Flick any specks of dirt and dust from the mount and face of the artwork with a soft brush. Then clean the glass, using a spray-on cleaner or a mixture of methylated spirit and water. Do this well away from the artwork and mount. Lay the glass on top of the mount, followed by the frame. Then turn the whole assembly over and place it face down on some newspaper, holding it firmly in place to prevent specks of dust from getting in.

Professional framers use a glazing gun to secure the backing board to the frame with special diamond-shaped metal "sprigs", and if you intend doing a lot of framing it may be worth investing in one. However,

Using a glazing gun

fine ½ in (1 cm) panel pins can be used instead. Drive them in horizontally to the inside of the frame with a pin hammer, sliding its head across the backing board. Each pin should be driven in by about half its length, making sure that it pinches the edge of the board tightly. Hold the frame against a batten clamped to the edge of your work surface while you do this. The batten will absorb the force of the hammer blows and prevent the frame from coming apart at the joints.

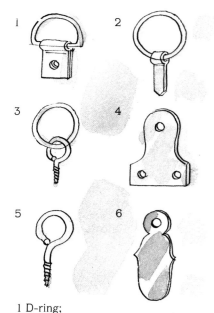

1 D-ring;
2 Back hanger;
3 Screw eye with ring;
4 Glass plate;
5 Screw eye;
6 Swing clip

If the assembled glass, mount, artwork and backing are so thick that they are flush with the back of the frame, the solution is to chamfer the edges of the backing board with a knife or rasp so that the pins can be driven into the side of the frame at an angle.

Sealing the frame

The back of the frame should be sealed to keep out dust and moisture which could damage the artwork. The best seal is provided by gummed paper tape. Make sure the tape is wide enough to make a complete seal between the backing board and frame. Cut four strips, wet them with a sponge and press them into position, overlapping the corners. Use a scalpel or sharp knife to trim the ends of the tape for a neat finish.

Hanging

Select hanging fittings according to the weight and size of the finished frame. It is no good hanging a heavyweight frame with lightweight fittings.

Simplest of all are screw eyes which are fixed into pilot holes made in the backs of the frame sides with a bradawl or thin drill bit. Position them about a third of the way down from the top. Then stretch picture wire or nylon cord between the eyes, making sure it is not completely taut, but at the same time not so slack that it will show above the frame when it is hung. A variation on the screw eye has a metal ring attached to the eye.

Screw eyes can split the wood of a thin frame so it is not advisable to use them on very narrow mouldings. In such cases use D-ring fittings which are attached to mounting plates and are intended for fixing to the backing board rather than the frame. They are very secure and have the advantage that they are completely hidden. Be sure to fit them to the hardboard before you assemble the picture in the frame. Again, they should be positioned about a third of the way down from the top and about a fifth of the width in from the edges using bifurcated rivets — some fittings have a single rivet hole, while those intended for heavy pictures have two. Holes for the rivets can be drilled or pushed through the board with a bradawl. The legs of the rivets are then inserted through the fittings and the holes in the backing board before being opened out flat on the inside. Cover them with fabric tape to protect the artwork.

If you want the frame to sit flush against the wall, use picture plates instead, fixing them either to the top edge or the sides of the frame with brass screws. The plates can then be screwed to the wall.

The normal type of wall fixing is the picture hook and nail, which should be driven in at a downward angle so that the picture wire sits against the wall. On old partition walls, particularly lath and plaster, it is advisable to identify the position of the timber framework behind and nail into that only. On brick or block walls be sure to use masonry nails. These can be bought with picture hooks already attached.

For heavier frames a screw driven into a plastic wall plug will be more secure. Always use two wall fixings for really heavy frames in order to spread the load.

O ften the idea of picking up an old frame for next to nothing from a junk shop and tidying it up may be more attractive than the thought of making a new one from scratch. There is no doubt that many old frames are well worth restoring. However, take care particularly with very old frames which may have a value in their own right as antiques. In some cases, amateur attempts at restoration may ruin them completely or reduce their value. Whenever you are dealing with something that is old it may be advisable to have the work done by an expert. Before carrying out any restoration work always consult a professional framer or antique dealer.

Where the frame is important to you purely for its visual appeal, there is no reason why you should not clean it up or take it apart and reglue it, or cut it down in size if you wish. Old veneered or natural wood frames will generally respond well to the simple application of good wax polish. General dirt and grime can usually be removed from a gilded or painted frame by wiping it over with a cloth moistened in white spirit (use an old toothbrush on intricate mouldings), but always test it on a small unobtrusive area of the frame first in case the finish is dissolved by this liquid. Never use water, as it can damage some finishes, or in the case of gold leaf, remove the finish altogether.

Over the years, the glass of a glazed frame may have acquired a thick film of dirt and the cardboard mount could well be stained and faded. In this situation, the glass can be cleaned and the mount replaced. Cut round any tape seal at the back of the picture with a sharp knife or scalpel to expose the pins or sprigs holding the backing board in place. Carefully pull these out with pliers and remove the backing, picture, mount and glass. If the picture is attached to the mount with tape, carefully ease a palette knife under the tape where it is attached to the mount to separate the two. Then trim the overlap of tape from the picture with a knife or scalpel.

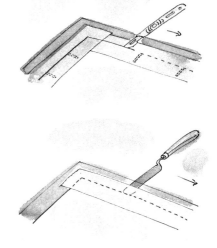

Dismantling the frame

If the glass is dirty, all that may be necessary is to wash it in soapy water or clean it with a proprietary glass cleaner. However, if this still won't remove all the staining, try using wire wool soaked in methylated spirit which will shift practically everything.

With the glass and inserts removed, the frame can be given a more complete cleaning and inspected for loose joints, rot or woodworm. If there are any signs of the last two, treat the frame with an appropriate fungicide or woodworm treatment, making sure it won't stain the surface of the moulding by applying it from the back. It is always worth discarding the old backing board and making a new one from hardboard. Old backing boards, particularly those in pine, are positively harmful to pictures.

If the joints are loose, gently ease the frame apart by clamping one length of moulding in a vice (protecting it with pieces of scrap wood) and gently tapping the adjacent piece away from it with a hammer and block of wood. If necessary, use pliers to work the corner pins out once you can get hold of them between the ends of the mouldings. Pull out all the pins and remove the old glue from the ends of the mouldings by carefully sanding with glasspaper wrapped round a sanding block. You must be very careful to hold the block flat against the ends of the mouldings, otherwise you will round them off and gaps will show at the corners when you remake the joints. If you bought the frame with the object of framing a picture other than the one that came with it, you could cut the frame down in size and re-mitre the ends, which would obviously remove the old glue at the same time. Then reassemble the frame using glue and frame clamps

as you would when making a new one (see pages 159–60). Drill fresh pilot holes for new corner reinforcing pins rather than using the old holes, which should be disguised with a little wood filler. The filler can be coloured by adding artists' powder paint when mixing it so that it blends in with the frame's finish.

If only one joint is loose you may be able to repair it or at least strengthen the loose joint without separating the lengths of moulding. One way is to gently ease the joint apart slightly with a blunt, stainless steel knife and work some fresh glue into it with the blade. Then clamp the corner and allow the glue to set. Alternatively, an L-shaped steel plate can be screwed to the back of the frame to hold the mouldings together.

If the frame has a painted or varnished finish which is in poor condition, you can remove the old finish with a proprietary paint stripper or sand it down with glasspaper to expose the grain of the wood. After washing off all traces of strip-

per, you can apply any finish you wish. Any nicks in the surface can be built up with wood filler and sanded to match the shape of the moulding, but if you intend staining the frame the filler will need colouring first to match the surrounding wood.

Most old gilded or painted frames have a base of gesso under the finish which disintegrates when wet. Gesso is a white plaster-like substance composed of chalk whiting and size and in the case of ornate frames is the material from which the mouldings themselves are made. If these gesso mouldings are loose or have fallen off altogether, reglue with ordinary woodworking glue.

If only small areas of moulding are missing, try repairing them yourself. Make a mould of the missing pieces by pressing plasticine or a similar substance to an area of the frame where the moulding is complete. Then press a modelling material such as plaster of paris or car-body repair paste into the mould and allow it to set. When

hard, remove the cast from the mould; or sand the bottom of the new cast flat and stick it in place with woodworking glue. Finish it with gold paint or whatever is appropriate to the original finish. If, however, a lot of the moulding is missing, it will have to be restored professionally. If you are advised that the frame is not worth restoring you might consider soaking the plaster off altogether. Old moulded frames usually have a sound wooden base which will make attractive frames in their own right.

If you are fortunate enough to have a frame with carved wood moulding, do not attempt any restoration yourself. It may be valuable and should be taken to a specialist furniture restorer.

Lacquer frames that are chipped, cracked or scratched can sometimes be restored successfully at home. If the original gesso underneath is intact, rub down with fine steel wool, then recoat either with another layer of gesso or with one of the new, easily applied fillers. Then apply tinted shellac — at least two coats — and finish with a transparent glaze.

Of course, if you buy an old frame, any picture that comes with it is likely to need restoration too.

Picture restoration is very skilled and you are more likely to ruin the picture than restore it. Always consult an expert.

Sometimes one buys a print, whether new or old, on paper that is distinctly waved. There is little that can be done about this without altering the value. If the print is precious, and the ripples unbearable, you must search out a paper conservator. If all else fails, he can paste the print onto an acid-free board and — if the job is done really well — the value will not be affected.

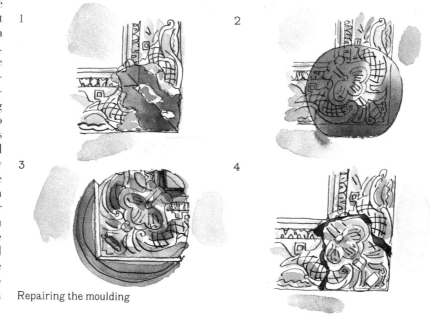

1 2 3 4

Repairing the moulding

Terms in SMALL CAPITALS denote cross-references.

Agate A semi-precious stone used by gilders to burnish GOLD LEAF to a rich finish.

Beading A narrow strip of wood used as an embellishment on a frame.

Bevel The sloped cut edge of a mount's "window".

Block mounting A process whereby a print or poster is mounted on a block of wood, usually chip board.

Bole Also known as French clay. A clay applied over a GESSO base as the ground for GOLD LEAF. It comes in various colours, which show through when the gilding is DISTRESSED.

Box frame A deep frame, usually of thin panels of wood, designed to display three-dimensional objects.

Burnish To rub gold or metal leaf with a gilder's AGATE burnisher until the leaf reaches a rich and brilliant finish.

Conservation board Mount board made from rag or specially treated woodpulp which is free from acids or other chemicals harmful to works on paper. Essential for mounting original works of art on paper. Also known as acid-free board/card.

Distressing To antique a painted or GILDED finished frame, so that the base coat shows through, giving an impression of age.

Double mount Two mounts used together, the window of the top one being cut larger to create a stepped effect.

Downlighter A light fitting that directs light downward, usually from the ceiling.

Dry mounting An adhesive method of attaching a picture onto a backing. A sheet of film is placed between picture and backing and heat is applied to fuse the two together.

Faux bois A decorative finish designed to look like wood, with whorls and knots.

Fillet A strip of wood sometimes used in frames to provide space between the picture and the glass cover.

Floating frame A frame for oil paintings which is separated from the canvas by a narrow recess, usually dark, giving the impression that the painting is floating within the frame.

Foxing Tell-tale small brown spots of mildew found on old prints and drawings.

Gesso Chalk whiting mixed with size and applied in layers to a frame before GILDING or other finishes are added.

Gilding Applying a gold finish – usually with GOLD LEAF.

Glaze To cover with glass; or to protect with a thin coat of varnish.

Gold leaf Paper-thin sheets of pure gold which can be applied to picture frames.

Gouache Opaque watercolour paint, in which the pigments are coarser, and usually extended with white pigment. Also known as body colour.

Hinge mount The correct form of mount for original works on paper. The window mount is attached to the backing card with a paper hinge; the picture is suspended from the backing card by a paper tab.

Limed wood Wood treated with thin white paint, GESSO or wax to give a lighter effect.

Marbling (or marbelizing) Decoration on paper or wood intended to resemble the mottled appearance of marble.

Marquetry Thin layers or inlays of VENEER applied, often in complex designs, to a wooden frame.

Mitre A 45° angle cut on a frame MOULDING, where each moulding section meets another at the corners.

Mitre box A metal or wood device used for cutting MOULDING at the correct angle for frame making.

Moulding Framer's moulding consists of strips of specially designed RABBETTED wood from which picture frames are made. Builders' moulding was originally designed for interior detailing, such as the trim or beading on skirting boards, but can be used for picture frames too.

Mount (mat in USA) The card surround normally used to protect and enhance artworks on paper. A window is cut in the card, beneath which the picture is placed.

Quadrant A strip of wood with a quarter-circle profile, sometimes used to form the RABBET of a picture frame.

Rabbet (or rebate) In a picture frame, the stepped edge which creates a slot for the mount, picture and glass.

Ragging The decorative painting technique by which a tinted glaze or WASH is applied over a base coat and then, while still wet, distressed with a crumpled rag to give the distinctive uneven effect.

Reverse frame A frame made of MOULDING which slopes away from the picture.

Scoop frame See SPOON FRAME.

Slip An inner frame, often made of wood and painted or covered with fabric, used as a protective and decorative barrier between the main frame and the picture, in the same way as a mount is used.

Spattering A decorative paint technique whereby the paint is literally spattered onto a base coat from the end of a stiff brush, giving a fine speckled effect.

Sponging A decorative paint effect whereby the paint is applied over a base coat and then, while still wet, dabbed with a natural sponge to give a mottled, cloudy effect.

Spoon frame A frame with a concave trough running along it. This type of frame is also known as a hollow or scoop frame.

Stippling A decorative paint effect whereby paint is applied over a base coat in short jabbing movements with the end of a short-haired stiff brush, giving an impression of overall fine dots.

Stretcher A jointed wooden framework over which the canvas of an oil painting is stretched taut and tacked.

Tempera A painting medium in which pigment is mixed in a water-soluble emulsion, usually egg yolk.

Uplighter A light fitting designed to direct light upward.

Veneer A thin layer of good-quality wood applied over a base consisting of less expensive wood.

Wash A coating of thinly diluted paint applied to obtain a translucent or delicate finish.

Wash line A WASH applied to a mount in a narrow or broad band, with defining ink or watercolour lines along either side.

White gold An alloy containing gold with platinum and palladium, and sometimes smaller amounts of silver, nickel or copper.

The following list of suppliers is selective, reflecting the author's personal experience. General framers are not recommended, as they are too numerous to choose from.

Arquati UK Ltd,
2 Wolseley Road,
Kempston,
Bedford MK42 7AY
Mouldings, mount boards (including conservation board), framing materials (wholesale only).

Ashworth & Thompsons Ltd,
12 Baron Street,
London N1

and
227 Granton Road,
Edinburgh EH5 1HD,
Scotland

and
42 Great Strand Street,
Dublin,
Eire

and
22 Duncrue Crescent,
Belfast, Northern Ireland

Berrick Bros.,
Paper Merchants Ltd,
Unit 1, Deptford Trading Estate,
Blackhorse Road,
London SE8
Mount boards (including conservation board), framing materials, specialist papers.

Design Animation Ltd,
16/17 Windsor Park,
Windsor Avenue,
London SW19 2RR
Perspex frames and display cases.

Falkiner Fine Papers Ltd,
76 Southampton Row,
London WC1B 4AR
Specialist papers.

Green and Stone Ltd,
259 Kings Road,
London SW3 5EL
Art supplies.

Lawrence and Aitken Ltd,
Albion Works, Kimberly Road,
London NW6 7SL
Mount boards (including conservation boards).

TN Lawrence & Son,
117-119 Clerkenwell Road,
London EC1R 5BY
Specialist papers.

Lion Picture Framing Supplies Ltd,
148 Garrison Street,
Bordesley,
Birmingham B9 4BN
Mouldings, mount boards, framing materials, framing equipment.

Magnolia Mouldings Ltd,
Magnolia House,
Rutherford Drive,
Park Farm South,
Wellingborough,
Northants NN8 6GS
Mouldings, mount boards, general framing materials, framing equipment.

Meridian Mouldings Ltd,
The Old Maltings,
Lombard Street,
Orston,
Nottinghamshire NG13 9NG
Mouldings, mount boards, framing materials, framing equipment.

Marpatt Reproductions Ltd,
Unit 3, Catherine Street Industrial Estate,
197 Gipsy Lane,
Leicester LE4 6RN

Paperchase Products Ltd,
213 Tottenham Court Road,
London W1A 4US

Reeves Art Shop,
178 Kensington High Street,
London W8 7RG
Art supplies.

Rose & Hollis,
98 Belgravia Works,
159/163 Marlborough Road,
London N19 4NF
Mouldings.

Rowney & Co Ltd,
12 Percy Street,
London W1A 2BP
Art supplies.

K. Scharf Ltd,
Britannia Road,
Waltham Cross,
Hertfordshire EN8 7NU
Mouldings, mount boards, framing materials and equipment.

D. & J. Simons and Sons Ltd,
120-128 Hackney Road,
London E2
Mouldings.

Sisslings Mouldings Ltd,
Merrydale Road,
The Euroway Estate,
Bradford,
West Yorkshire
BD4 6SD
Mouldings, mount boards, framing materials, framing equipment.

Winsor and Newton,
51 Rathbone Place,
London W1P 1AB
Art supplies.

ANTIQUE FRAME DEALER
Colin Lacy Gallery,
203 Westbourne Grove,
London W11 2SB

REPRODUCTIONS AND ANTIQUE FRAME RESTORATIONS
John Davis Framing Ltd,
8 Bury Street,
London SW1Y 6AB

John Tanous Ltd,
115 Harwood Road,
London SW6 4QL

SPECIALIST CONSERVATION FRAMERS
Piers Feetham,
475 Fulham Road,
London SW6 1HL
Also specializes in hand-finished and decorative frames.

Trumpington Gallery,
52 High Street,
Trumpington,
Cambridge CB2 2LS

ACKNOWLEDGMENTS

The authors would like to thank the following people for their invaluable help and advice:

IMAGES AND SURROUNDS
Jane Gordon Clarke of Ornamenta who designed the rooms featured on pages 13 (right): 28 (bottom left) and 29 (top): David Ashton-Bostock for the interior shown on page 20: Jancis Robinson. who supplied the picture shown on page 22: Ornamenta for supplying the picture shown on page 28 (bottom left): and Cork Street Framing for the framing and print shown on page 28 (bottom right) and on page 29 (top).

THE PROFESSIONALS AT HOME
Special thanks go to the seven designers who allowed their homes to be featured and many of whose interiors appear elsewhere throughout the book: Christophe Gollut. Derek Frost. Liz Macfarlane. Nina Campbell. Daniel and Claude Meiller. Jane Churchill. Mario Buatta.

THE FRAMER'S PORTFOLIO
Dillinger and Wallace for the flowers in the sections on Introducing Mounts and Treatments for Mounts: Timney Fowler for the fabric used in Bold Mounts: Colin Lacy for supplying the antique frames: Ian Mankin for supplying the fabrics for Fabric Mounts and Slips: Diane Mercer who made some of the mounts and gilded frame samples: Olivia Stanton who made some of the bold mounts: Lucinda Thomas for making some of the lacquer samples. Many of the samples were specially made by Piers Feetham.

PICTURES IN SITU
In addition to interiors designed by the seven featured designers. we should also like to thank the following designers for allowing us to show some of their interiors: Amelia St George who did the stencilling in the room shown on page 98 and the stencilled mounts on page 139 (right) and Cork Street Framing for supplying the Piranesi prints and frames for the former and the frames for the latter: Charles Hammond. who designed the room featured on page 110. photographed by Andrew Kolesnikov: Jo Robinson of Mrs Monro Ltd. whose home appears on pages 111 and 113: David Ashton-Bostock who designed the interior shown on page 124: John Campbell Picture Frames Ltd for supplying the prints and frames shown on page 139 (left):

Linley Sambourne House featured on page 142. 147 (top left) and 148 (right). We also gratefully acknowledge the kind permission of the Raymond O'Shea gallery. featured in Learning from the Print Room on pages 25 (middle top and bottom) and 150–1.

PRACTICALITIES
Thanks to Ian Penberthy for his contribution to this section.

In a book whose theme is pictures. unfortunately it is impossible to acknowledge each artist individually. but we would like to thank all those artists whose works appear in these pages.